All New Real-Life Case Studies for Teachers

WILLIAM HAYES

ROWMAN & LITTLEFIELD EDUCATION
A Division of
ROWMAN & LITTLEFIELD PUBLISHERS, INC.
Lanham • New York • Toronto • Plymouth, UK

Published by Rowman & Littlefield Education
A division of Rowman & Littlefield Publishers, Inc.
A wholly owned subsidiary of The Rowman & Littlefield Publishing Group, Inc.
4501 Forbes Boulevard, Suite 200, Lanham, Maryland 20706
http://www.rowmaneducation.com

Estover Road, Plymouth PL6 7PY, United Kingdom

British Library Cataloguing in Publication Information Available

Library of Congress Cataloging-in-Publication Data

Hayes, William, 1938–
  All new real-life case studies for teachers / William Hayes.
    p. cm.
  ISBN 978-1-60709-142-4 (cloth : alk. paper) — ISBN 978-1-60709-143-1 (pbk. : alk. paper)
  — ISBN 978-1-60709-144-8 (electronic)
  1. Teachers—United States—Case studies. 2. Teaching—United States—Case studies. I. Title.
  LB1775.2.H386 2009
  371.100973—dc22   2009019861

Printed in the United States of America

Contents

Foreword

First-year teachers' survival is far from assured. Teacher educators sending their graduates into the real world can only hope that they will survive the rigors of the first year. Insulated by the college campus environment, students may construct excellent lesson plans and under the protection of a master teacher deliver highly viable learning experiences during their student teaching. Nevertheless, the very best students leaving quality teacher preparation programs are not assured of an easy, comfortable entry into the profession. The risk level for first-year teachers is very high. And after surviving the first year, the statistics demonstrate that new teacher survival out to five years is not predictable.

While teacher preparation programs can make every attempt to prepare their graduates for the hazards of the real world, the school environment can present the new teacher with perplexing dilemmas at the least and career-ending nightmares at the worst. Attempts to provide authentic learning experiences in schools of education that simulate the school environment and culture fall far short of portraying the volatile culture of the school.

Is there a way to increase the first-year teachers' probability of success? Bill Hayes's work provides a means to prepare the new teachers for their first encounter with the real world. He masterfully crafts case studies that pinpoint the issues. He combines the key factors that generate each issue into a rich and compelling storytelling.

The realism for anyone with school experience is striking. As each case study unfolds, experienced instructors will see, hear, and smell the school in their mind's eye. Bill's case studies, in the hands of the skillful instructor, can generate a truly authentic experience for the students without leaving the college classroom.

The twenty-four case studies cover the most likely dilemmas found in schools and school districts in this day. The breadth of the offerings serves as an indicator of the expansive dynamic of the school culture. Exposure to the case studies will provide the student with an opening to the complexity and comprehensiveness of the school system.

While the stories taken together can be somewhat overwhelming, taken one at a time, they can give the instructor the opportunity to carefully unravel the factors at play. Students will be able to see how those factors contributed to the issue and how it might have been prevented in the first place. They will also be able to analyze and evaluate possible steps to take to resolve the issue.

The case studies Hayes has so artfully developed provide a means to heighten students' resiliency. Unfortunately, in some variation, the broad array of issues Hayes presents in his case studies are likely to occur in the future, and some may very well be encountered by the new teacher. Or it is very possible that the new teacher will be confronted by an issue not among those Hayes has illustrated, but, after examining and exploring the case studies offered by Hayes, the new teacher may have identified and adopted ways and means that can be called on to deal with issues not previously encountered.

Teaching is demanding work requiring the ability to analyze new, unique, troubling, and even threatening issues, and then to respond appropriately. If we are to increase our students' success in their initial encounter with the school culture, we need to provide them with awareness of the possible issues they will face. They need to have looked in depth at the issues and rehearsed ways to respond to them. Hayes's case studies provide the materials for just that. They provide authentic circumstances, to be examined in the security of the classroom.

Dr. James H. Frenck
PLC Associates, Inc., An Outcome-Driven Consultancy

Acknowledgments

There are a number of people to thank for helping to prepare this book. First and foremost is Sharon Bligh, a student assistant in the Teacher Education Division at Roberts Wesleyan College. Along with typing the entire manuscript, she has assisted in the research and the editing. Sharon has been a true partner in this project. Unlike the first edition of *Real-Life Case Studies for Teachers*, I have included "Additional Resources" for each case study. These have all been prepared by Linda Jones, who is our college's director of reference and bibliographic instruction. There is no question in my mind that they enhance the book and provide sources that will be helpful to both students and instructors. Several of my teaching colleagues have also assisted in developing ideas for the book. I am particularly grateful to Dr. Gary Debolt, Marty Garland, and Professor John Campoleito. Finally, as with my previous twelve books, my wife Nancy has proofread every page and has offered helpful suggestions that have improved the final product. I am indebted to all of these individuals for their interest and support in the completion of this project.

Introduction

As a teacher of both undergraduate and graduate education students, I use case studies as an essential component in all of my classes. After every semester, students have written in their course evaluations that reading and discussing these real-life dilemmas faced by teachers was usually the most helpful aspect of the courses. Students seem to appreciate the opportunity to think about and discuss authentic practical problems faced by today's teachers. Using case studies is not unique to the field of education. A similar approach is utilized in preparing students in business, law, accounting, and medicine. Although most professors choose to use a traditional text as well, case studies make teaching the topics in the text come alive for students.

In 1999, I wrote two books of case studies. One was designed for administrators and the other for teachers. A year ago, I completed a book of updated case studies for future school administrators titled *Real-Life Case Studies for Administrators*. This volume has been well received and is being used in a number of colleges and universities. I believe that a new book of case studies for teachers would also be helpful.

During the past decade numerous new issues have arisen that affect a teacher's work. Developments such as No Child Left Behind, an increase in student dropout rates, increased student diversity, and inclusion have greatly impacted what is occurring in schools. With this in mind, I have sought input from current classroom teachers and administrators to help me identify those topics that are most important for today's teacher. This book is written for students at every level and can be used with college freshmen as well as graduate students. Another way that case study books are being used successfully is with in-service programs for teachers. Principals and other administrators are using them, especially with new teachers in their district. The case studies can be part of an orientation program for new teachers or for a district-wide class available to all teachers.

In my own classes, I have attempted to align the cases with topics that I am discussing as part of the curriculum. Students are asked to read the case studies and answer the questions at the end of the chapter. These questions provide the basis of discussion not only concerning the specific dilemma outlined in the case, but also the larger issues that are raised in the chapter. As a special feature of this book, I have added a section to each case study called "Additional Resources." This allows faculty and students to seek out articles dealing with the topic of the case.

It is my hope that those who read this book or implement it as part of a class will benefit from the consideration of the problems raised by the cases. There are no easy answers to the questions that follow each chapter, but they are presented in the hope that they will induce true reflection on how to deal with these problems that will be faced by those of us engaged in the teaching profession.

1

Is a Pay-for-Performance System a Good Idea for Schools?

What Is the Best Way to Pay Teachers?

During the 2008 presidential campaign, both Senator John McCain and Senator Barack Obama supported the idea of rewarding excellent teachers. Neither candidate was specific in how this should be done. They are not alone in calling for change in the way teachers are compensated. Board of education members, especially those who work in the private sector, often raise the question: Why can't teacher salaries be determined using the same methods we find in the business world?

Historically, teacher unions have had serious reservations about such an approach, usually pointing to the difficulty of fairly evaluating the effectiveness of individual teachers. Most often, the imposition of any such system would need to grow out of the collective bargaining process and, as a result, agreement has been rare. Still some districts have agreed on a plan or at least a system in which merit is part of the teacher compensation plan. It would appear that the issue will continue to be discussed at the federal, state, and local levels. This case study deals with such a dialogue taking place in a school district.

When the minutes of the last board of education meeting were posted in the faculty room, one item quickly became a topic of heated discussion among the teachers at the Glendale Secondary School. Buried in several pages of minutes was a motion that read as follows:

It was moved by Allen Davenport and seconded by Susan McLeavitty that prior to the upcoming teacher negotiations, the board of education should seek to gain

3

the agreement of the Glendale Teachers Association to establish a joint task force made up of teachers, board members, and community members to study a possible means to include a "pay-for-performance plan" in the next teacher contract.

The motion was unanimously passed by the board. Allen Davenport explained that he wanted to develop a system acceptable to teachers, and this could best be done by a joint committee meeting before the formal negotiations began. If such an agreement could be reached, the issue would not become a roadblock to an overall settlement.

A new board member, Allen was the vice president for personnel of a chain of small-town banks. He was very familiar with compensation systems used in private industry and saw little reason why such a plan could not be used in schools. A decade earlier, the school district had talked about what was then called "merit pay," but the teachers union had held out until the proposed method for compensating teachers was dropped by the board of education. Following the posting of minutes, the motion dealing with a pay-for-performance plan quickly became a topic of discussion in the faculty room. Mary Leavitt, a first-year teacher in the district, was fascinated by the conversation.

The first person to comment after hearing the motion read was a veteran English teacher, who quickly reacted to the idea by confidently predicting, "It will never happen—there are too many variables in trying to judge our kind of work. What are they going to do, give us raises based on the test scores of our students?" Mark Saladius, a member of the biology department, interrupted: "Results on test scores depend on the students you are assigned. I have one class of future dropouts who could care less about tests. The best teacher in the world could not get many of these kids to pass a state biology test."

Virginia Thompson, a teacher of math, agreed that using test results should not be the primary method for judging a teacher's work, and instead pointed to the system used by her husband's accounting firm. It appeared to Mary that the fact that Virginia's husband had just received a $5,000 merit bonus seemed to make her more open to the idea. Sylvia Lopez, a member of the Spanish department, asked, "How does your husband's company decide on bonuses?" Virginia explained that her husband's boss used a specific grading plan to evaluate all of her subordinates.

A member of the art department, Sean Heath, responded by suggesting that he would not want "our illustrious principal" deciding on his salary. He related that the principal, Robert Hector, admitted after one class observation that he didn't know anything about art. The only thing that he suggested in his lesson evaluation was that the class had been a bit loose in allowing students to talk and get out of their seats while they were working. For Sean, it seemed that his boss did not understand that an informal atmosphere could enhance student creativity and that students should not be forced to remain silent and in their seats while doing an assignment. As far as judging student artwork, the principal did not seem to appreciate anything that didn't look like a photograph. Two of the projects that seemed to bother him were both awarded prizes in the county art contest. Sylvia agreed and pointed out that their principal knew little or no Spanish and that he could not fairly judge whether students were truly learning the language.

Social studies teacher Joey Rotini had been quiet during the discussion, but then raised another possibility. He asked, "What about judging each other? My colleagues in my department are in the best position to determine the most effective social studies teachers." Mark pointed out, "We talked about that possibility ten years ago during the merit pay discussions, and the fear was that it would be bad for morale. Right now most of us are friends and we work well together. If we were judging each other, it could introduce serious competition, politics, and stress within the department. This would not be good for our school culture."

Not willing to give up, Joey said, "Well, then, how about using student evaluations? At least at the high school level the kids are mature enough to contribute input on our teaching effectiveness." This caused a buzz in the room, and three individuals began to talk simultaneously. Once order was restored, Virginia Thompson observed, "Even in high school, students would be too heavily influenced by how entertaining a teacher was in class." Another teacher said that they also would be affected by the grades that they received in the course and observed that a student receiving a C or a D was unlikely to rate a teacher highly. It was also pointed out that such a system might only add to grade inflation. The third teacher weighing in on the suggestion argued that students know even less than a principal about what is or is not good teaching.

Mary Leavitt, the first-year teacher, had been listening carefully to the entire discussion and had found it rather depressing. On first hearing about "pay-for-performance," she had found the idea appealing. She had thought often about the fact that her salary was less than half of that of several veteran members of her department. At least one of these teachers, she was convinced, was less effective than she was in the classroom. Mary believed that whatever measure was used, she would be ranked higher than a number of experienced teachers. It just didn't seem fair that faculty members' salaries were dependent only on their years of experience. When Mary left the faculty room, she decided to think about the issue and maybe try to devise her own suggestion for a pay-for-performance plan.

The next day she saw a poster on the bulletin board announcing that there would be an open meeting of the union to discuss the organization's position on a possible pay-for-performance task force. Mary wondered whether she should attend the meeting and perhaps share her ideas about the topic.

DISCUSSION QUESTIONS

1. Share your thoughts on each of the following possible ways to judge teacher effectiveness:
    a. student test scores
    b. evaluations done by supervisors
    c. evaluations done by teaching peers
    d. student evaluations
2. If you were to devise a system that you felt would work the best, what might it be?
3. Do you support the use of the pay-for-performance concept in the teaching profession?
4. Should Mary Leavitt support the idea at the upcoming open meeting of her union?

ADDITIONAL RESOURCES

Carr, N. "The Pay-for-Performance Pitfall." *American School Board Journal* 195, no. 2 (February 2008): 38–39. Retrieved November 11, 2008, from Professional Development Collection database.

Dillon, N. "The Merit Scale." *American School Board Journal* 195, no. 4 (April 2008): 28–30. Retrieved November 11, 2008, from Professional Development Collection database.

McMahon, M. "Performance-Based Salaries" (pp. 1-1). Great Neck Publishing (2008). Retrieved November 11, 2008, from Research Starters–Education database.

Schaubroeck, J., J. Shaw, M. Duffy, and A. Mitra. "An Under-met and Over-met Expectations Model of Employee Reactions to Merit Raises." *Journal of Applied Psychology* 93, no. 2 (March 2008): 424–34. Retrieved November 11, 2008, doi:10.1037/0021-9010.93.2.424.

The Boy Crisis

Is There a Problem with the Achievement of Boys in School?

Both *Time* and *Newsweek* magazines have carried cover stories that highlighted what appears to be a national trend showing boys lagging behind girls academically in many public schools. Where educators once worried about girls, especially in the fields of math and science, it is now the boys who may be underachieving. This is especially true in schools located in urban and some poor rural areas. For many years young women have scored well, especially in English, but today it seems that they are outstripping the boys in almost every area. While some scholars and organizations have not accepted this as a problem, more and more teachers and administrators have begun to take the issue seriously.

Phillip Bligh, a math teacher in the Maple Hill High School, was very much interested in a column he had come across in his local newspaper. The article, written by an African American journalist, Clarence Page, was titled "Helping Boys without Hurting Girls." Sitting in his empty classroom during his third-period break, Phillip was looking at a sheet of paper on which he had scribbled the following notes from Page's column:

- The days of fretting over lagging girls' achievement have faded into a "Boy Crisis."
- Boys are more likely than girls to arrive at the very highest and very lowest math scores. Girls are more likely than boys to score well overall and arrive in the top 5 percent of math scores.

- Stories and statistics describe unmotivated, easily distractible boys who are falling behind in test scores, forgetting their homework, or, when they finish it, are either forgetting to turn it in or are unable to find it in their disorganized backpacks.
- These problems are particularly acute for black males. The Schott Foundation for Public Education, an educational think tank in Cambridge, Massachusetts, found that fewer than half of black male students across the country are graduating from high school.
- Black students are performing best in states like North Dakota and Vermont where there are the fewest black students. Alternatively, where white males are trapped in under-resourced schools like Indianapolis and Detroit, they performed as poorly as or worse than black males.
- Boys are performing most poorly in areas where more of them are raised without strong male role models at home. Growing numbers of boys of all races are growing up without fathers at home because of divorces, separations, and out-of-wedlock births.
- Boys tend to learn in ways quite different from the ways of girls. Some experiments in school choice and single-gender education are beginning to show results, although experts continue to debate the overall statistical results.[1]

As he considered the notes he had made, he began to think about the situation with his own students and all of the others enrolled at Maple Hill. It occurred to him that the boys in his own ninth- and tenth-grade math classes might fit into the pattern described in the article. They were enrolled in an urban school that had over 70 percent minority students, most of whom were African American. The building was located in a city with a high rate of poverty. Phillip had heard someone in the administration quoted as saying that 85 percent of the students were eligible for free or reduced-price lunches.

The information in the column caused him to take out his grade book and compare the grades of the boys and girls in his present classes. Despite the fact that a handful of boys were earning excellent grades, the bottom 25 percent of his students were overwhelmingly male. Another thought crossed his mind as he recalled that at last year's graduation ceremony, eight out of the ten top students recognized were girls. He also remembered reading a list that contained the names of the graduates who were attending college. Pulling out that list from a pile of papers on his desk, he saw that almost 70 percent of the acceptances were for girls. While a number of boys were going to attend excellent colleges, the list of the schools the girls were attending was even more impressive. Farther down the same document were the names of the students enlisting in the military. This list was predominantly made up of boys.

After doing this preliminary investigation during his study hall, Phillip decided that he would that evening go through his entire ten-year career as a teacher and determine whether or not there was a trend regarding gender of his former students. After staying up well past his bedtime he concluded that there well may have been a growing problem with the boys in his math classes. Using his skills in statistics, he was able to show with his own classes that there had indeed been a reduction in boys' final exam grades, while the girls were doing slightly better.

The next day after school, he went to the guidance office to talk to his friend Scott Rodgers. When he showed Scott the results of his mini-study as well as a copy of the Page column, his colleague's reaction was, "I'm not surprised." Scott shared his own challenge as a father of attempting to have his son take his classes seriously. He noted that other boys, who would be considered "good kids" by the faculty, were also more interested in sports, computer games, and skateboarding than they were in homework.

On the other hand, Scott said his fourteen-year-old daughter had already decided that she wanted to be a doctor. She had looked into how one might get accepted into a medical school and had already identified several colleges she wanted to consider. When they concluded their discussion, neither man was totally convinced that this was indeed a problem in their school. More important, they were even less certain of what to do if this was an issue in their district.

Because they had access to the transcripts of all of the current and past students at Maple Hill High School, it would not be hard for Scott and Phillip to do an in-depth study of student grades, not only in math but in other subjects as well. Phillip said that he could help with the math aspect of their joint project. It would take a lot of time, but they were both intrigued by the issue. Two weeks later, after many hours of after-school work, they concluded that there had been a rather discernible change in how boys and girls were doing academically in their school. During the ten years they had considered, there were increasingly more boys in the bottom 25 percent of their class.

Despite the fact that a significant number of young women had dropped out of school due to pregnancy, the percentage of boys quitting school had greatly surpassed the girls and had consistently risen. They also found that during the last nine years, the number of girls in the top ten academic students had been increasing. Both Phillip and Scott were now convinced that their school should be concerned about the fact that the female students were outstripping the male students academically in the classroom. They also agreed that identifying the problem was much easier than finding the solution. Having completed their study, both men were unsure what to do with the data they had gathered.

DISCUSSION QUESTIONS

1. Was it your experience in school that the girls were more serious about academics than the boys in your classes?
2. What, if anything, should Phillip and Scott do with their findings?
3. Do you think single-gender schools would be a positive step toward attempting to improve the achievement of boys? Why or why not?
4. What can schools and individual teachers do to help with this perceived problem?

NOTES

1. C. Page, "Helping Boys without Hurting Girls," *Kitsap Sun*, kitsapsun.com/news/2008/aug/22/clarence-page-helping-boys-without- hurting-girls.

ADDITIONAL RESOURCES

Pearce, R. A. "Parenting Matters in the Achievement of Boys, Girls." *The Morning News* (September 11, 2008). www.nwaonline.net/articles/2008/09/11/news/091208azuaspkrs.txt.

"Raising Boys' Achievement." Cambridge University Faculty of Education, 2002. www-rba.educ.cam.ac.uk.

Sax, L. "The Boy Problem: Many Boys Think School Is Stupid and Reading Stinks." *School Library Journal* (September 1, 2007). www.schoollibraryjournal.com/article/CA6472910.html.

There Is Not Enough Time in the Day

One Result of No Child Left Behind

Teachers all over the United States would agree that the No Child Left Behind law has had a major impact on their schools. Because of the emphasis on language arts, math, and, to a lesser degree, science, one of the results of the legislation apparently has been to reduce the amount of time teachers are spending on other subjects. This is especially true in grades 3–8, where language arts and math tests are mandated at every grade level. Schools have attempted to find additional time in the school day to emphasize these areas. According to a number of studies, this has resulted in less instructional time for social studies, music, art, and physical education. In addition, teachers reported that they have been eliminating activities such as field trips, guest speakers, and special projects. This case study tells of how one group of elementary teachers is attempting to deal with the pressure created by the standardized tests.

The school year had just begun, but the fifth-grade team at the Hamilton Central Elementary School was already feeling the stress caused by their principal's comments at the opening meeting for teachers. Following this full faculty meeting, each grade-level team had met to discuss how they were going to deal with the new demands in language arts. At their team meeting the four teachers talked about how to find time for all of their subjects in a weekly schedule. The session ended without a plan but not without a unanimous sense of frustration among the group.

After the initial faculty meeting, all of the teachers in the school were talking about the new reading program. Their young second-year principal, Kevin Grant, had worked with a consultant and several teachers over the summer to select a new language arts program. The fact that the previous year's reading scores had placed Hamilton Elementary School near the bottom of the county schools had caused the superintendent to order her new principal to do something about those scores beginning that summer. Kevin had quickly formed a committee, and they met with a number of sales representatives and made a selection.

Together with the company representative, the committee had spent three hours at the opening faculty meeting introducing the new program. There were to be a series of after-school meetings to train the faculty during the first semester. Because they were somewhat overwhelmed with the initial presentation, the teachers were happy to hear that the new program would not be used with the students until the second semester. Even with this assurance, a number of the faculty members were uncomfortable with what they had heard at the meeting. For these critics the new program seemed overly structured and encumbered by the need to administer frequent tests and to maintain a complex record-keeping system.

A number of the veteran teachers in the school had already shared their opinion that this new approach would greatly limit them in teaching lessons that in the past had enriched their language arts program. One teacher observed that she would become merely an actor with her lines already scripted by the teacher handbook. Her colleague added the observation that the new program would take all of the creativity out of teaching. None of these criticisms had been the primary topic in the fifth-grade team meeting. For these teachers, it was the principal's announcement that, beginning immediately, all grade levels would be required to allot two and a half hours each day solely to teaching language arts. The fifth-grade teachers calculated that for them, this would be an increase of almost three hours a week.

The evening following the team meeting, Jodi Smith had lain awake in bed replaying in her mind the principal's mandate to add time for language arts instruction to the fifth-grade schedule. The team member who had been the most upset was their experienced team leader, Karen Williams, a twenty-six-year veteran teacher in the district. Karen was perhaps the most respected member of the faculty, not only within the school but also within the community. She had been quick to point out in the team meeting that the most obvious place to reduce instructional time was in the area of social studies and perhaps science. Jodi had quickly pointed out that under No Child Left Behind there was at least one required test in science at the elementary level. Even though that test was not given until the sixth grade, it was unlikely that it would be easy to steal minutes from the limited time currently allotted to science education in fifth grade.

Jodi then remembered that at this point in the discussion she had raised the possibility that the school could reduce the time allotted for music and art classes. This had brought a quick response from Karen, who said, "I would fight any suggestion that we cut these areas. For some students, these classes are the best part of the school day." A third member of the team, Brett Tobin, said that he would rather cut music and art than social studies. He felt strongly that what is currently being taught in our American history and government units is essential not only for preparing students for middle school and high school, but also in ensuring that the students become good citizens.

At that point in the meeting, Jodi remembered that she had then raised the possibility of reducing the time spent in physical education. It was Karen who had responded that the two days each week currently allotted to these classes was not even close to what the state required. She told the group, "Our school is already fudging the requirement by claiming that there is physical activity each day during the lunch hour and at recess." The fact was that there was often no break in instruction, except for lunch, and the lunch period was not long enough for extended time on the playground. When the weather was bad, the students were forced to remain in the cafeteria.

The fourth member of the team, Amber James, had been quiet until this point in the meeting. Although she had been listening carefully to the other teachers, she had been searching through a pile of papers she had in front of her. When she did choose to contribute to the conversation, she shared with the group an article she had found. As a former New York City resident, she still subscribed to the New York Times, and read to the group a portion of the article she had saved. In recalling what Amber had quoted, Jodi remembered that it referred to a study finding that "71 percent of the nation's school districts had reduced the hours of instructional time spent on history, music, and other subjects to open more time for reading and math."[1] Amber went on to suggest that one reason for the drastic reductions is clear, especially in her former hometown. In New York City teachers are being evaluated by their students' test results.[2]

At this point Jodi had interjected, "We have forgotten all about math. Remember that our fifth-grade math scores were almost as bad as those in reading, and we certainly cannot find extra time by stealing it from math. If anything, we might have to add to the time we spend teaching math." Brett, who cared deeply about social studies, then concluded, "We are back to social studies, and that seems to be true throughout the nation. I remember reading a quote in an education magazine by someone from the National Council for Social Studies who said that 'the worst thing that ever happened to social studies has been the No Child Left Behind Law.'"[3] Karen talked about an article in the *American Teacher* pointing out that schools that had once allowed band and chorus rehearsals during the school day were now scheduling them before and after school. According to this article, the same was true for release time for instrumental music lessons.[4]

Karen then raised the concern about the special activities that their fifth-grade team had carried out in the past. She mentioned specifically the Occupation Day, when the students' parents came to school to talk about their jobs. This caused Jodi to think about the time devoted to their field trips to the aquarium and historical museum. Someone else had mentioned the Pioneer Day they had sponsored annually. Actually, the fifth-grade classes spent the better part of a week preparing for a day when the students, teachers, and many parent volunteers would engage in various activities of Native Americans and pioneers during the nineteenth century. All of the teachers were more than aware of the amount of instructional time devoted to these projects and activities. They also knew that for their former students, these days were the most memorable during their year as fifth graders.

Jodi became even more upset when she realized they might have to cancel their annual spring activity known as the Junior Olympics. This was an event that saw the entire school spending a day on the athletic field in various competitions, ranging from class tug-of-wars to the hundred-yard dash. Every class represented their favorite country and did a preliminary study about that nation. They prepared an appropriate lunch with a favorite food from that country and made flags and banners that were part of the morning parade along with a short ceremony that began the competition. Parents and grandparents brought their lawn chairs to become spectators for the various events. Amber expressed all of their feelings when she said that "giving up all of these things to raise reading test scores a couple of points just is not worth it."

Before Jodi drifted off to sleep that night, she concluded that no one on her team was enthusiastic about the new language arts program and that they were all extremely apprehensive about trying to rearrange their schedule to accommodate the additional time for language arts. All summer she had looked forward to starting a new school year, but the faculty meeting and the session with her fifth-grade colleagues had cast a negative shadow over the year to come.

DISCUSSION QUESTIONS

1. Do you think the increased emphasis on language arts, math, and, to a lesser degree, science is having a negative impact on the overall school program?
2. One solution to this problem is to increase either or both the minutes in a school day or the days in the school calendar year. Do you think this is a good solution? Why? Why not? Do you think such extensions will happen in most school districts? Why? Why not?
3. If you were in the position of the fifth-grade team, how would you suggest approaching the problem of increasing the time devoted to language arts instruction?

NOTES

1. S. Dillon, "Schools Cut Back Subjects to Push Reading and Math." *New York Times*, March 26, 2006, www.nytimes.com/2006/03/26/education/26child.html (accessed September 18, 2007).

2. J. Medina, "Teachers to Be Measured Based on Students' Standardized Test Scores." *New York Times*, October 2, 2008, nytimes.com/2008/10/02/education/02teachers.html (accessed October 2, 2008).

3. Dillon, "Schools Cut Back Subjects to Push Reading and Math."

4. R. Whitehorne, "NCLB: Taking a Toll on Arts and Music Education." *Philadelphia Public School Notebook*, Summer 2006, www.thenotebook.org/editions/2006/summer/nclb21.htm (accessed September 13, 2007).

ADDITIONAL RESOURCES

De Oliveira, L. "History Doesn't Count: Challenges of Teaching History in California Schools." *History Teacher* 41, no. 3 (May 2008): 363–78. Retrieved November 14, 2008, from Academic Search Premier database.

Nathan, L. "What's Been Lost in the Bubbles." *Educational Leadership* 66, no. 2 (October 2008): 52–55. Retrieved November 14, 2008, from Academic Search Premier database.

Weingarten, R. "Accountability That Works." *Education Week* 32-32 (May 14, 2008). Retrieved November 14, 2008, from Academic Search Premier database.

What Is Fair, What Is Right?

Athletic Eligibility for Special Education Students

High school teachers have additional concerns with regard to assigning grades as a result of the eligibility policies in their schools. Most high schools have some sort of plan in place to ensure that athletes, and often participants in other extracurricular activities, keep their grades at an acceptable level to participate in these programs. Although such policies vary greatly from district to district, they are very common. Teachers are often placed in a situation where the grade they assign to a student could make that student ineligible for a team or for participation in another extracurricular activity. When a faculty member is placed in such a position, there is sometimes pressure on the teacher to show some sympathy for the student in question. Such a dilemma could be made even more difficult if the young person involved is classified as a special education student.

Chelsey Kenney is a second-year math teacher at Oak Ridge High School. While sitting at her desk after school, she had repeated her calculation for Andrew Evens's math grade for the third time. Every time it had come out at 62 percent, and it was clear to her that such a percentage had to be converted to an F on the boy's five-week report. Her system for reaching the grade had been announced to the students on the first day of class. In addition, Chelsey had handed out a written description of her grading process. After her first year of teaching she had become convinced that her grading system should be as objective as possible, as there were always students and sometimes parents who might question a grade lower than what they had hoped for.

The plan she had devised was quite simple. Homework papers, which she graded carefully, were to be counted as 25 percent of the overall grade. Weekly quizzes and a unit test would account for the other 75 percent. With the five-week progress reports due in the office tomorrow, she had used her computer grading system to average the homework grades. Having just finished grading the unit test, she had assigned the results of the exam as 40 percent of the grade while the quiz grades were to be counted as 35 percent.

On calculating Andrew's grade, she found that he had earned a passing grade for the homework but a failing grade when she averaged in the quizzes and unit test. The resulting average of sixty-two, when converted to an F, would be enough under the Oak Ridge eligibility system to make him ineligible for the next five weeks, or until the teacher reported that he was passing the course. Chelsey had followed the eligibility policy very carefully for all of her students. After the third week of classes, she had sent out seven warning notices. Students, as well as their parents, were informed that if the grades did not improve by the end of the five-week marking period the students would be placed on the ineligibility list.

Only two of Chelsey's students failed to raise their grades. Eva Smith was an average student who, because of personal and home problems, had missed thirteen days of school during the first five-week period. There was no question that her missing homework and poor quiz grades would result in a failing grade for the math course. For her, ineligibility was the least of her problems, as she was not a participant in any sports or extracurricular activities. Chelsey had made it a point to have a personal conversation with Eva and felt that perhaps the worst was over and that soon Eva would be able to concentrate more on her schoolwork.

On the other hand, ineligibility for Andrew would be a serious matter, not only for him but for the Oak Ridge football team. As a senior, Andrew was a three-year veteran of the varsity team. He was one of two players who played on both the offensive and defensive squads. On the offensive team he was a tight end who had already caught twenty-one passes during the first four games. Perhaps even more important to the success of the team was his position on defense. A ferocious defender, he played middle linebacker and was the leading tackler on the squad. Weighing close to two hundred pounds and standing over six feet tall, Andrew was an imposing figure on and off the football field. Along with being very strong, he had also been named to the all-conference track team, where he won the county championship for the hundred-yard dash.

Despite his considerable athletic talents, Andrew had learning difficulties that had made his years in school an ongoing struggle. This was particularly true in the area of mathematics. Diagnosed in elementary school with dyscalculia, he had been classified in fourth grade as learning disabled. Chelsey had learned that his disability was related to dealing with numbers. It is similar to dyslexia, which causes students to reverse their letters when reading. Andrew had a similar difficulty with numbers.

Up until now the boy had managed to barely pass his math classes with the help of a resource room teacher. Now in his senior year, he was taking algebra for the second time in Chelsey's class. This course was one that his school and state required for graduation. During his first weeks in class he had gone faithfully to Jack Miller's resource room for help with his homework. Although his papers were sometimes difficult to decipher, Chelsey found them most often deserving of a passing grade. The same was not true with the regular quizzes she gave her class. Even with the extra time granted by his individualized education plan, Andrew almost always failed these quizzes.

Whether he would earn a passing grade at the end of the five-week marking period seemed to have come down to earning a passing grade on the heavily weighted unit test. Because she was worried about her students, she asked him several times during the days preceding the test whether he needed any extra help. Andrew said this option was not necessary, as he would be working with Mr. Miller.

Having now graded the tests and calculated the class averages, Chelsey knew she only had until the end of the next school day to turn in her grades. At that point she decided to take a few minutes to talk to Jack Miller about Andrew. When she asked him if Andrew had come for help prior to the exam, she was shocked to learn that he had not shown up. She was told that Andrew had promised to come in during his free period, but it turned out that his coach had asked him to report to the school trainer to do some exercises for his knee, which had been slightly injured during the last game.

The coach, Mark Munoz, a physical education teacher in the building, had earlier shown an interest in Andrew's academic progress, and Chelsey guessed that he did not know that the sessions with the trainer might interfere with Andrew's preparation for the algebra unit test. After talking with

Jack she went back to her classroom, where she was surprised to find Coach Munoz waiting for her.

The football coach began the conversation by reporting that Andrew had told him that he thought that he had "blown the algebra test." On hearing this, Coach Munoz could not help but wonder if the results had been as bad as his player thought. When Chelsey told him the test results and how the final average had come out, the coach was obviously disturbed. He related how Saturday's game was against the school's biggest rival and that there would be three thousand people there to cheer on their favorite team. This game, he said, was a "big deal in the community," as it was a rivalry that went back seventy-five years. He also pointed out that for Andrew it was important in that several scouts from local community colleges would be there specifically to watch him play. It was possible that these colleges would offer him a football scholarship to pay for his two years at a community college. This would be extremely helpful to his family, as they had very little money to pay college tuition for their four children.

The coach went on to make it very clear to Chelsey that her decision on eligibility would make a significant difference in Andrew's future. When she told him that the boy had chosen to go to the trainer rather than to get help in algebra, the coach agreed that his athlete should have known better and he went on to apologize for not knowing about the potential conflict. Before Coach Munoz left her classroom, he advised Chelsey to talk to Matthew James, the principal, about her dilemma. Chelsey knew that Mr. James was a great football fan, as she had watched him be an enthusiastic cheerleader during the school's pep rallies. If he became involved, and that seemed possible, Chelsey guessed that he would be sympathetic to Andrew and to the team.

On the other hand, she knew that if it were any other student probably no one would have said much about eligibility. If she somehow rationalized a way to raise the student's average, she couldn't help but wonder if she was sacrificing her standards to avoid potential problems with those individuals who thought it important to have Andrew participate in the weekend's game. More than the one game, as she also thought that his ineligibility could well extend until the end of the season. The only way he would be taken off the list prior to the issuance of report cards, at the end of the quarter, would be if she notified the office that his work was now passing. It was questionable, if based merely on homework assignments and a quiz or two, that Andrew could easily raise his average before the next unit test.

There was one other person she wanted to talk to about Andrew. Rebecca Seiger was her friend and informal mentor. As a special education teacher, she might have some insight on Andrew as a special education student. The fact was that in the past, Rebecca had worked with Andrew. In an earlier discussion she had shared her opinion that Andrew usually worked hard enough to pass his courses, but there was no question that his true interest in life was athletics. While he always had difficulty as a student, he had gained popularity with his fellow students and many of the faculty for his feats on the football field and the track. Chelsey doubted that he would ever get through even a community college if he did not get much more serious about his classes.

Even though Rebecca said that the boy did not work as hard as he could, she reminded Chelsey that his disability was real and that it made math extremely difficult for him. When Chelsey asked her friend whether the fact that he was classified as a special education student would affect the eligibility issue, she was disappointed to learn that the boy was expected to receive a regular high school diploma and would be covered by all of the rules just like the other students. The only difference was that he was given special services as a result of his individualized education plan. This meant that Andrew would receive assistance from Jack Miller and extended time for tests.

After leaving her friend's room, Chelsey could think of no one else to talk to about her problem. Since the decision did not have to be made until tomorrow, she decided to pack up her books and papers and think more about the problem after she arrived at home.

DISCUSSION QUESTIONS

1. Do you believe that academic eligibility policies are helpful at the high school level?
2. Do you think any or all classified special education students, who are included in the regular classrooms, should be exempt from such policies?
3. What should Chelsey do about assigning a math grade to Andrew?

ADDITIONAL RESOURCES

Bukowski, B. "A Comparison of Academic Athletic Eligibility in Interscholastic Sports in American High Schools." *The Sport Journal* (2001). www. thesportjournal.org/article/comparison-academic-athletic-eligibility-interscholastic-sports-american-high-schools.

Godek, J. "Inclusion for Students on the Autism Spectrum." *School Administrator* 65, no. 8 (September 2008): 32–36. Retrieved November 21, 2008, from Professional Development Collection database.

Reeves, K. "Athletic Eligibility: Right or Privilege?" *The School Administrator* (November 1998). www.aasa.org/publications/saarticledetail. cfm?ItemNumber=4565.

Helicopter Parents

Parents Who Are Too Involved

Although much of the literature identifies a large number of the so-called helicopter parents as baby boomers (parents born between 1946 and 1964), there is reason to believe that the issue is likely to survive among their children, who have been labeled the "millennial parents" (born 1982 to 1995). It is also true that in any generation there are parents who are excessively active in the lives of their children and are thought by others to hover over them. But the issue has been much more prominent in recent years. Not only can such parents create a problem for teachers and school administrators, but in some cases their behavior can cause psychological problems for their children. Besides hindering a student's development of independent habits, a parent who is overly protective can create additional stress in their children's lives. In recent years teachers have been exposed to numerous articles and workshops on how to deal with such parents; still, one can never understand the difficulty of dealing with such a situation until it is experienced firsthand.

Samantha Strevy, a second-year eighth-grade social studies teacher at the Copper Hills Middle School, had heard the term "helicopter parent" but had never really experienced the issue either as a student teacher or during her first full year of teaching. It was only the third week of September, and she now realized what was meant by the term. The realization came during a lunchroom conversation in the faculty cafeteria during which Samantha had mentioned that she had received three e-mails from Mrs. Switzer that day. After hearing about the e-mails, it was her friend, Harrison Johnson, who labeled Mrs. Switzer a helicopter parent.

It seemed an appropriate label for someone who had already e-mailed Samantha at least twenty-five times during the first month of school. The problem today concerned the first unit test that Samantha had handed back yesterday. Ben Switzer had taken the corrected exam home, and Mrs. Switzer was very unhappy that her son had earned only an A- on the test. The exam had consisted of twenty multiple choice questions, four short essays, and one extended essay. The first e-mail this morning had dealt with one of the multiple choice questions, which Mrs. Switzer thought was confusing, and she argued that the response her son had chosen was equally valid with the choice Samantha had considered the correct answer.

In her message Mrs. Switzer had looked up the issue in an older textbook to argue her point. Samantha had taken the question from the test bank that was published with her newer text and after receiving the e-mail had gone back to her book to the appropriate chapter. It was a chapter her students had been assigned to read, and in her response to the unhappy parent she cited a sentence in her book that supported her answer. An hour and a half passed, and then the second e-mail arrived.

This time the unhappy parent was contesting the points that had been awarded to her son on the extended essay. The question asked the students to explain and evaluate the primary weaknesses in the original document adopted by the Constitutional Convention in 1787. Ben had received twenty-eight points out of a possible thirty for his answer. During the time between her two e-mails Mrs. Switzer had visited the home of Ryan Zifchock, who was in the same class, and asked Ryan's mother if she could see her son's social studies exam. Mrs. Switzer had chosen this particular parent because Ben had mentioned Ryan had earned 100 percent on the exam. Ryan's mother hesitated but did agree to look in her son's room for the exam and found it on his desk.

Mrs. Switzer asked to look through it. After comparing the two papers, she had e-mailed Samantha saying that she thought Ben's essay was superior to Ryan's and that she could not see why her son had not been given full credit on the essay. Samantha remembered why she had taken off two points on Ben's answer. For her and for the textbook, the fact that the original constitution contained a compromise that counted slaves as three-fifths of a human being was a major weakness of the original document. In responding to Mrs. Switzer, she expressed her opinion that any of the students writing the essay should have included this weakness in order to receive full credit.

It was five minutes before lunch when Samantha received her third e-mail from Mrs. Switzer. This time the tone was much sterner. It began with the information that Mrs. Switzer had a minor in American history from Colgate University and that she disagreed with Samantha's position on her son's test. The message went on to say that she had called the director of social studies education in the district and had made an appointment to see him later that week. Samantha knew that if she had agreed to give the boy two more points his grade would have gone from an A- to an A. That would have probably solved the problem with Mrs. Switzer for now. Still, she believed that her decisions regarding the test were valid and she wasn't ready to change the grade. At the same time she could not help but wonder what her boss would have to say when Mrs. Switzer attempted to coerce him.

Unfortunately, Mrs. Switzer was not the only parent Samantha was dealing with who might deserve the label of helicopter parent. The two situations could not have been more different. Mari Adams was physically disabled and confined to a wheelchair. A victim of an automobile accident several years earlier, she had made what appeared to be an excellent adjustment to her disability. Mari was a fine student and was well liked by her classmates. Many of them made a point to seek her friendship, and there always seemed to be a fellow student eager to assist her when it appeared necessary.

Mrs. Adams had spent the entire first day of classes that year with her daughter and attended all of her classes. After that she visited the school several times a week to talk with each of Mari's teachers. During these frequent conversations she always asked whether other children were picking on her daughter. Samantha had seen no indication that there was any problem, but Mrs. Adams continued to raise the issue during her frequent visits. She was also extremely concerned about how her daughter was doing in passing from one class to another. All of Mari's teachers assured the worried mother that Mari was always on time for class. There were also frequent questions about the quality of Mari's homework assignments. In Samantha's class they had always been done extremely well.

One day recently when Samantha had complimented her student on a particular paper, she found out why the papers were always of such high quality. The homework was always written by Mari, but the girl confessed that her mother and father both worked with her on every assignment and that Mari was actually copying the first draft of the homework that her mother had written.

The situation had become even more complicated the previous week when Samantha met Mr. Adams for the first time. If possible, he seemed even more concerned about his daughter than his wife did. Mr. Adams had heard that Mari had been one minute late to Samantha's social studies class the day before, and he was extremely concerned that this lateness would be held against her. The fact was that Mari and her friend had been late to class because they had been talking to a group of friends in the hall. Samantha had treated them just as she would any other student who came to class late. She had merely reminded the girls that it was important to be in their seats when the bell rang. Mr. Adams said that he had come to school to remind Samantha that his daughter was disabled and that teachers needed to be more sensitive to his daughter's disability. As Samantha thought back on the incident, she was sure that neither of the girls had been surprised or bothered by her words regarding their lateness to class.

In thinking about dealing with Mrs. Switzer and the Adams family, Samantha could not help but think that this could be a long year unless she dealt with the problem now.

That evening she decided that she would attempt to do some research to try and find out how to best deal with helicopter parents. She was shocked when her Google search turned up over seventy-six thousand sources. They included network television shows and articles in publications ranging from news and education journals to larger pieces dealing with history and psychology. Because it was an issue that she would likely have to deal with more than once in her career, Samantha decided to print a number of the articles and learn what she could.

DISCUSSION QUESTIONS

1. Is it likely that this issue of "helicopter parents" will be one that teachers in the future will have to deal with? Why? Why not?
2. What should Samantha do about her situation with Mrs. Switzer?
3. How should Samantha deal with Mr. and Mrs. Adams?
4. In both cases, would it be wise to talk with the students involved? Why? Why not?

ADDITIONAL RESOURCES

Reddin, N. "Parents Invade the Workplace." *Des Moines Business Record* 42-42 (October 20, 2008). Retrieved November 21, 2008, from MasterFILE Premier database.

Shellenbarger, S. "Helicopter Parenting: A Breakdown." *Wall Street Journal—Eastern Edition* 250, no. 74 (September 27, 2007): D1-D1. Retrieved November 21, 2008, from Academic Search Premier database.

Strauss, V. "Putting Parents in Their Place: Outside Class." *Washington Post* (March 21, 2006). www.washingtonpost.com/wp-dyn/content/article/2006/03/20/AR2006032001167.html

6

The Ongoing Debate on Block Scheduling

Is Block Scheduling Just Another Fad?

Block scheduling for secondary schools has been a subject of continuing controversy for over two decades. Before that, an even more sophisticated approach to organizing the school day, called modular scheduling, had been introduced in some schools. Proponents of class periods lasting longer than the traditional forty-five minutes have argued that the extended time allowed greater flexibility to teachers and students. There is no single agreed-upon block schedule, but rather a wide range of options that allow a school to develop a plan that best meets its educational needs. Although numerous studies have attempted to judge the effectiveness of various scheduling options, there still is not a consensus on the best scheduling plan for secondary schools. Because of this, discussions continue in schools across the country as they attempt to find the plan that will serve them best.

Harry Anderson had been a math teacher at Pine Hill High School for the past twenty-four years. He felt that he had earned a positive reputation in the school and the community as an effective instructor. During his long career he felt that he had earned the respect of his students, their parents, and most of his colleagues. Lately, however, he was becoming increasingly aware that a number of the newer teachers in the building viewed him as part of the "old guard." For them, he was sure that he was seen as a very traditional teacher who might be too set in his ways.

It was true that in recent years he had shared his reservations concerning the school district's large expenditure on classroom computers. He did not see the advantage of doing grading and attendance on the computer as particularly helpful. He also sometimes resented the constant barrage of e-mails that he received on his classroom computer. At a recent faculty meeting he had suggested that the administration, as well as everyone else, should talk to others directly rather than always sending e-mails. In his brief tirade at the meeting he shared the number of administrative e-mails he had received during the previous month. Although he did not use any names, he mentioned e-mails from fellow teachers who were only steps away from his classroom. Harry was fairly certain that comments such as this were marking him as someone who was opposed to new things.

Personally he felt that this viewpoint was unfair. After all, he was currently using PowerPoint in his classes and had made the transition to using the computer programs for grading and attendance. When he could not find a parent at home by using the telephone, he had even resorted to e-mailing the family when he wanted to communicate a problem or sometimes even tell a parent what a fine job their child was doing in his classroom.

On the other hand, the announcement at this afternoon's faculty meeting had truly upset him. The school's new principal, Carol Jones, had announced that she intended to establish a committee to study the possibility of creating a block schedule for Pine Hill High School. The thirty-three-year-old administrator had mentioned how she had enjoyed such a schedule, not only during her own high school years but in her previous position in another school as the assistant principal. Working in that school, which had had a block schedule for ten years, only solidified her view that this was the best kind of plan for any secondary school.

The idea of creating a block schedule only brought back unpleasant memories for Harry. It must have been at least a dozen years ago when another principal had raised the possibility of devising a new schedule. At that time Harry had chaired the faculty committee that had considered the issue. Not only was he the chairperson of that committee, but, as it turned out, he led the opposition to any change in the school's traditional seven-period day. After what seemed an exhausting study, the committee had voted five-to-four not to support the change. The group had been unable to agree on any specific plan to present to the faculty, and as a result a motion to end any further study of the issue passed in the committee by a single vote.

The committee's decision did not end the debate. The principal, as well as a number of the faculty who supported the idea, raised the issue at a full faculty meeting. This session turned out to be the longest meeting that Harry could remember in his twenty-four years at the school. He could not help but recall that it was after 5:30 when he made the motion that the committee's recommendation be accepted and that further study of block scheduling should cease. Following his motion there was an additional twenty minutes of heated debate. A motion to table the issue until the next meeting was made but failed when thirty-one of the fifty-eight teachers present voted against tabling the issue. This was followed by a motion calling for the question that was passed by a similar vote. Someone then called for a roll-call vote so that every member of the faculty would be on record as to how they voted. Even this did not end the discussion, as someone now made a motion that the principal and his two assistants should be allowed to vote on the motion. This had led to an even more heated exchange, and a majority of the faculty agreed that it was unprecedented for the administrators to have a vote. The final count, when it was taken, saw thirty teachers in favor of ending the discussions on block scheduling and twenty-eight opposed.

This final vote was something of an anticlimax given the earlier votes. It seemed unreal that Harry could remember so well this entire meeting that took place more than twelve years earlier; but he not only remembered the voting, he was now recalling some of the arguments that had been put forward. He could even remember who was on each side of the controversy. In opposing block scheduling his most significant ally had been Lucas Hernandez, the chair of the school's small foreign language department. Lucas's primary argument against the idea was that with foreign language students it was important that the students be exposed to and speak the language as often as possible rather than merely two or three days a week. When the group considered a schedule that would meet every day, Monday through Friday, for an extended period every semester, Lucas had worried that a student might take Spanish I the first semester of their freshman year and not be enrolled in Spanish II until the following year. He felt that this would be a disaster for his students, as they might forget much of what they had learned. The fact was that he felt that forty-five minutes of Spanish five days a week was the best possible arrangement for his classes.

Harry had fully supported his friend's arguments. During his career his approach to teaching math had not changed. The class would begin by reviewing the homework assigned the previous day. Frequently he would have the students put their work on the chalkboard, and he would point out any errors. When he was sure the class understood the assignment, he would then introduce the new lesson. Harry was proud of the fact that he was now using PowerPoint along with the chalkboard to present this new work. Recently he had also experimented with the SMART Board but was not yet sure how he felt about using this new device to help him with his lessons.

After he explained the new work for the day, the students would be given time to practice working on appropriate examples. Harry would move around the classroom to help individual students with the work. Again, if time permitted, he would have some students put their work on the board. At some point before the period ended, he would give the class their assignment for the next day. Should there be any time left, the students would be allowed to begin their homework. Although there were days when he was rushed for time, over the years he had become adept at doing everything he wanted to accomplish during a forty-five-minute period.

Harry and Lucas also had allies in the music department. Several of the music teachers had heard stories from other districts where block schedules had resulted in reduced time for the music ensembles. They learned that in several schools the groups had been forced to meet either before school or after school for band and chorus rehearsals. At the end of the school day, there were frequently conflicts with other extracurricular activities such as student council and the yearbook. Worst of all was the possible problem of forcing interscholastic athletes to choose between participating on a team and being a part of the band, chorus, or orchestra.

While Harry, who was the chairperson of the math department, had been able to convince his entire department to vote against a new schedule, the science department had been solidly in favor of longer periods. They had argued that they would be able to teach a formal lesson and follow it with a related laboratory experience on the same day. This would provide a continuity that was not possible with forty-five-minute periods, as there was not enough time to do both. The result was that the labs were scheduled on a totally different day. In order to accommodate both the lecture and lab in one period, they secretly hoped that because there were only eighteen lab stations, the school would be forced to reduce their science class sizes.

The art department had also been unanimous in their support of the block scheduling. For them the prospect of extended periods would give their students more time to work on their projects. They argued that because it took a significant amount of time for students to get out their materials and to later clean up, the longer classes would give more uninterrupted time to students.

Although the math teachers, language department, and music faculty had voted against block scheduling, their votes were for the most part canceled out by the science and art teachers. Faculty members in the other departments had split their votes. Some social studies teachers had thought that they could use the additional time for discussion and special projects. Other more traditional teachers preferred meeting with their classes every day for forty-five minutes. As Harry remembered the debates, it occurred to him that the physical education and industrial arts departments were also split in their voting on the proposed schedule change.

As he thought about the crucial committee meetings prior to the voting, he began to recall some of the arguments that were put forward. Each side of the controversy had brought in the results of research studies as well as numerous articles that included both the advantages and disadvantages of block scheduling. Harry had actually kept a folder of some of these articles, and he found a page with his notes that included a summary of the main justifications for and criticisms of the longer classes. His notes mentioned the three possible options for an extended schedule. They were as follows:

- In the alternate-day schedule students and teachers meet every other day for extended time periods rather than meeting every day for shorter periods.
- In the 4/4 semester plan students complete four "year-long" courses that meet for about ninety minutes every day during a ninety-day semester.
- Students take two or three courses every sixty days in a trimester plan to earn six to nine credits per year.[1]

He also had notes on what might be considered the advantages of block scheduling.

- When students attend as many as eight relatively short classes in different subjects every day, instruction can become fragmented; longer class periods give students more time to think and engage in active learning.

- A schedule with one relatively short period after another can create a hectic, assembly-line environment.
- A schedule that releases hundreds or thousands of adolescents into hallways six, seven, or eight times each school day for four or five minutes of noise and chaotic movement can exacerbate discipline problems.
- Teachers benefit from more usable instructional time each day because less time is lost with beginning and ending classes.[2]

The final section of his notes summarized the major disadvantages of a block schedule, which were as follows:

- Many teachers continue simply to lecture students rather than engaging them in active learning. Block scheduling in itself is no guarantee of active learning. And if active learning doesn't take place during, for example, a ninety-minute class period, students may have trouble paying attention for the entire class.
- Student absences create problems under block scheduling. Making up missed work is always difficult. When a student misses one day of classes under block scheduling, the student misses the equivalent of two days of instruction under the traditional system. A weeklong absence means the student misses two weeks of material. Such an absence may cause a student to fall behind to the extent that making up the work is difficult.
- Teacher absences may lead to other problems, according to doubters. Under block scheduling, will a substitute teacher be qualified to teach ninety-minute periods of, for example, physics?
- With the semester plan for block scheduling, courses like languages or mathematics can be a problem. Because they are sequential, some critics point out that a student may take French I in the fall and not take French II in the spring, take nothing in the summer, and then take French II the following fall.[3]

Harry also remembered that one teacher claimed that the typical block schedule would actually result in less instructional time. One of the alternatives they were considering at the time was a schedule calling for eighty-five-minute periods. The teacher had pointed out that two forty-five minute periods were being traded for an eighty-five-minute class every other day.

The idea of reliving this divisive debate was one that Harry really wished to avoid. At the same time he knew that the current faculty at Pine Hill High School was much changed after twelve years. He was not at all sure that a new study of block scheduling would result in the same outcome. There were many young teachers, who, like the new principal, might have had a favorable experience with block scheduling. A faculty committee today might well be able to agree on a specific proposal, and it could also be easier to gain a majority vote for such a plan. He could not help but wonder if his new principal, Mrs. Jones, knew of the previous attempt to introduce a block schedule. It seemed likely that someone had told her about the potential for conflict her initiative might cause among the faculty.

The first decision Harry had to make was whether or not to sign up for the committee. He still believed that the idea of longer classes was merely an educational fad and that adopting such a schedule would have little or no impact on student learning. As he considered his long teaching career, he was sure that many of his students had greatly appreciated his classes and his teaching methods. He could remember a number of students who had gone on to colleges as math majors. In fact, he could name at least six of his former students who were now math teachers themselves. Harry treasured several letters he had received that had identified him as the primary reason students had gone on to study math. He was sure that having forty-five-minute periods had not hindered his teaching.

Still, he wondered if he was up to another fight over this issue. Perhaps more important, he could not help but ask himself whether he was indeed a reactionary who was standing in the way of progress. In his twenty-four years he had seen a number of educational fads introduced and eventually disappear. The idea of block schedules was still around, and maybe it did have some merit. One alternative for him was to be quiet this time, and, if it happened, he would learn to live with it. Perhaps it was time for the new generation of Pine Hill teachers to assume the leadership.

The more he thought about it, the more convinced he became that he should consider becoming involved. Perhaps he could do so with a more open mind than in the past. That night he would make a point of doing a search of current articles on block scheduling and try to determine if there was new research that clearly validated the approach. Based on that, he thought he could better make a decision on what he should do.

DISCUSSION QUESTIONS:

1. What, if any, experience have you had with block scheduling? If you have had the opportunity to be in a school with such a schedule, have you become a supporter or a critic of such schedules? For those without experience, do you have a positive or negative feeling toward block scheduling?
2. Give your primary reasons for either being supportive or in opposition to block scheduling.
3. If you were in a position similar to Harry's, would you seek to be a member of the committee and become actively involved in the new study?

NOTES

1. S. Cromwell, "Block Scheduling: A Solution or a Problem?" *Education World*, October 20, 1997, www.educationworld.com/a_admin/admin/admin029.shtml (accessed October 23, 2008).

2. "Block Scheduling: A Solution or a Problem?"

3. "Block Scheduling: A Solution or a Problem?"

ADDITIONAL RESOURCES

Matthews, J. "Class Schedulers Think Outside the Blocks." *Washington Post* (March 10, 2008). www.washingtonpost.com/wp-dyn/content/story/2008/03/09/ ST2008030901472.html

Merritt, R. "Block Scheduling" (pp. 1-1). Great Neck Publishing (2008). Retrieved November 21, 2008, from Research Starters–Education database.

An Autistic Student in a Regular Classroom

The Issues with Including Autistic Children

In February of 2007, the *Washington Post* published an article carrying the headline, "1 in 150 children in U.S. Has Autism, New Survey Finds." The article went on to estimate that this could mean that 560,000 children in our country were suffering from autism. It is described as a "poorly understood behavior syndrome" that "varies mysteriously from state to state." There are those who would question the validity of this finding given the fact that "there is no simple test to provide a definitive diagnosis." Not only is the condition difficult to diagnose, but scientists have yet to agree on how the condition is caused.[1]

Most authorities would agree that "there is probably no single gene or genetic defect that is responsible for Autism. Researchers suspect that there are a number of different genes that, when combined together, increase the risk of developing Autism." There also seems to be a connection between autism and certain medical conditions, as well as the possibility that "environmental factors and exposures may interact with genetic factors to cause an increased risk of Autism in some families."[2] Along with these factors, there have been those critics in recent years who have believed that the mercury preservative in vaccines has been a cause. This explanation has yet to be proven, and the vaccine makers have attempted to remove any possible risk.[3]

Whatever the cause, the number of students identified as autistic continues to grow, and these students become an increasingly larger percentage of those receiving special education services. This, of course, raises new challenges for teachers, as many of these children are being placed into inclusive classrooms.

The first four months of Katie Williams's return to the teaching profession had already been quite challenging. Beginning next month, it was bound to become even more difficult. Katie had taught for three years and then taken off the next thirteen to raise a family. Her first experience as a teacher in the Buchwald School District had been in a kindergarten classroom. Fresh out of college, she had been extremely enthusiastic about her job and loved all of her five-year-old students. Her classroom was a place where the children experienced music and art along with their regular curriculum. An accomplished pianist, Katie was able to enjoy accompanying her kindergarten singers on the piano. Her memories of working in kindergarten were all very positive.

When her own children had reached an age when she felt that they were old enough to not need her at home all day, Katie began to think about returning to teaching. During her years away from the school she had continued to volunteer as both a Girl Scout leader and Sunday school teacher. When she heard that her school district had a vacancy at the fourth-grade level, she visited her former principal who had told her, "When you are ready to return to teaching, come see me." Katie knew that the principal, Mrs. Dayton, had very much appreciated her work as a kindergarten teacher and she was very encouraged when Mrs. Dayton seemed to still remember her as a fine teacher. After going through the application process and interview, Katie and her husband were delighted when she was offered the fourth-grade position.

It did not take long for her to learn that there had been changes at the school and that the fourth-graders were different from the kindergarteners she remembered. Among the biggest changes was that she had two students who had been identified as in need of special education. Both had individualized education plans, IEPs, which required her to give them a great deal of individual attention.

One of the boys, Justin, had multiple physical disabilities and was confined to a wheelchair. Katie found that especially during transitions from one activity to another, she needed to help Justin maneuver. The other special education student was Kara Jacobson. Kara was a student who had been identified with a learning disability as well as attention deficit hyperactivity disorder. Because of her dyslexia, she was more than two grade levels behind in reading.

The fact that Katie spent so much time helping these students was brought to her attention by two parent volunteers during a field trip to a local museum. In a conversation following the trip, the parents had sympathized with her because of her difficulties in accommodating these children. They went on to ask whether having these children took away from the time she could spend with the "normal children." Actually, there probably would have been no problem on the field trip had her special education consultant teacher been able to participate; but because she was only scheduled for six hours a week with Katie, it was impossible for her to spend the full day on the field trip. It worried her that the parents might think that the teacher was neglecting their children because of the needs of the special education students.

The fact was that Katie was still somewhat uncomfortable meeting the IEP objectives of her two special education students. She was truly alarmed when Mrs. Dayton informed her that she would be assigned a new student with autism. Because she already had the two special education students, her class size was smaller than any of the other fourth grades, and it was not surprising for her to be assigned a new student.

Knowing that this would be a major new responsibility for Katie, Mrs. Dayton informed her that she would also be assigned a full-time aide and that her special education consultant would work half-time in her classroom. Although Katie was happy to hear about the extra help, she was not altogether comfortable with having to now deal with her newly assigned colleagues. During her first teaching experience in the kindergarten she had never had an aide and was not totally sure of the appropriate role of a person in this position.

Thus far, her work with Barb Davenport, her twenty-four-year-old, second-year special education consultant, had been somewhat difficult. Despite her limited experience, Barb was quite assertive. The fact that Katie had no formal training in special education caused Barb to think of herself as an expert specialist. She was not in the least bit shy in advising her older colleague, and at times Katie had felt as if she were Barb's student.

She could not help but think that her newly assigned full-time aide would also be something of a challenge. Mandy Ward was in her mid-sixties, had raised four children, and proudly let others know that she had thirteen grandchildren. Although they had never worked together, Katie also had observed that she was not a retiring and quiet personality. This was obvious when one watched her working with children.

Prior to meeting with either Barb or Mandy, Katie decided to find out as much as she could about autism. She began by going to one of her favorite websites to identify the symptoms of the disorder. It was clear that they varied from individual to individual, but the notes that she had taken listed the "core symptoms" as the following:

Social interactions and relationships. Symptoms may include
• Significant problems developing nonverbal communication skills, such as eye-to-eye gazing, facial expressions, and body posture.
• Failure to establish friendships with children the same age.
• Lack of interest in sharing enjoyment, interests, or achievements with other people.
• Lack of empathy. People with autism may have difficulty understanding another person's feelings, such as pain or sorrow.
Verbal and nonverbal communication. Symptoms may include
• Delay in, or lack of, learning to talk. As many as 40 percent of people with autism never speak.
• Problems taking steps to start a conversation. Also, people with autism have difficulties continuing a conversation after it has begun.
• Stereotyped and repetitive use of language. People with autism often repeat over and over a phrase they have heard previously (echolalia).
• Difficulty understanding their listener's perspective. For example, a person with autism may not understand that someone is using humor. They may interpret the communication word for word and fail to catch the implied meaning.
Limited interests in activities or play. Symptoms may include
• An unusual focus on pieces. Younger children with autism often focus on parts of toys, such as the wheels on a car, rather than playing with the entire toy.
• Preoccupation with certain topics. For example, older children and adults may be fascinated by video games, trading cards, or license plates.
• A need for sameness and routines. For example, a child with autism may always need to eat bread before salad and insist on driving the same route every day to school.
• Stereotyped behaviors. These may include body rocking and hand flapping.[4]

The source went on to say that some of these symptoms could be evident during a child's first three years. Although the problems created by autism were significant, she was happy to read that "with early and intensive treatment, most children improve their ability to relate to others, communicate, and help themselves as they grow older. Contrary to popular myths about children with autism, very few are completely socially isolated or 'live in a world of their own.'"[5]

Another website, www.familydoctor.org, listed the common signs of autism. They included the following:

- avoids cuddling or making eye contact
- does not respond to voices or other sounds
- does not respond to his or her name
- does not talk or does not use language properly
- rocks back and forth, spins, or bangs his or her head
- stares at parts of an object, such as the wheels of a toy car
- does not understand hand gestures or body language
- does not pretend or play make-believe games
- is very concerned with order, routine, or ritual and becomes upset if routine is disturbed or changed
- has a flat facial expression or uses a monotone voice
- injures himself or herself or is unafraid of danger[6]

Still another source cautioned against making generalizations about the possible symptoms of autism. In a publication from *Autism Speaks* she found the following information.

Autism is a spectrum disorder, which means it manifests itself in many different forms. A diagnosis can range from mild to severe, and though children who have it (i.e., are on the spectrum) are likely to exhibit similar traits, they're also as individual as the colors of a rainbow, each one managing a grab bag of symptoms. While one child may rarely speak and have difficulty learning how to read and write, another can be so high-functioning he's able to attend classes in a mainstream school. Yet another child may be so sensitive to the feel of fabric that all tags must be cut off before he wears a piece of clothing, while his friend who's also autistic may not have any sensory issues at all.[7]

In addition, Katie was interested in how the disorder was diagnosed. What she learned was that "having a child diagnosed with autism can be a devastating experience for many parents and families."[8] At the same time she was glad to read that there were support groups and specialized counseling available to parents and caregivers. Unfortunately, there seemed to be an issue as to whether various health insurance plans would pay for such services. Having learned about the symptoms, she could not help but agree with another source:

> There is no lab test or x-ray that can confirm the diagnosis of autism. The diagnosis of autism is based on clinical judgment regarding observations of the individual's behavior. Information from family members and other observers is of primary importance in making the diagnosis; however, the pediatrician may order tests to rule out other conditions that might be confused with autism, such as mental retardation, metabolic or genetic diseases, or deafness.... The comprehensive evaluation of a child with autism might include complete medical and family history; physical exam; formal audiology evaluation; selected medical/lab tests on an individual basis; speech, language, and communication assessment; cognitive and behavioral assessments; and academic assessment.[9]

It was sobering for Katie to read in another source that "autism is a lifelong disease that ranges in severity from mild cases in which the autistic person can live independently, to severe forms in which the patient requires social support and medical supervision throughout his or her life."[10] As to the treatment of the disorder, she had noted the following:

Appropriate early intervention is important. Once the diagnosis has been made, the parents, physicians, and specialists should discuss what is best for the child. In most cases, parents are encouraged to take care of the child at home. Special education classes are available for autistic children. Structured, behaviorally based programs, geared to the patient's developmental level have shown some promise. Most behavioral treatment programs include

- clear instructions to the child
- prompting to perform specific behaviors
- immediate praise and rewards for performing those behaviors
- a gradual increase in the complexity of reinforced behaviors
- definite distinctions of when and when not to perform the learned behaviors

The same source went on to say,

Parents should be educated in behavioral techniques so they can participate in all aspects of the child's care and treatment. The more specialized instruction and behavior therapy the child receives, the more likely it is that the condition will improve.

Medication can be recommended to treat specific symptoms such as seizures, hyperactivity, extreme mood changes, or self-injurious behaviors.

The autistic child requires much of the parents' attention, often affecting the other children in the family. Counseling and support may be helpful for the parents.

The outlook for each child depends on his or her intelligence and language ability. Some people with autism become independent adults. A majority can be taught to live in community-based homes, although they may require supervision throughout adulthood.[11]

After doing her research, Katie felt a bit more prepared for her new student, who would be joining her class at the beginning of next week. Mrs. Dayton had promised that the student's IEP would be arriving as early as tomorrow. When Katie had asked whether the student's former school had considered putting the child in a self-contained special education classroom, Mrs. Dayton reported that the administrator in the former school had said that the parents were adamant that their son be placed in a regular classroom. Katie could not help but think that several of the parents of her other students might not appreciate a new special education student in their children's classroom. The fact was that she was more worried about the parents' reaction than how her students would accept their new classmate.

In any case, she knew that both Miss Davenport and Mrs. Ward would be eager to talk with her about their new assignments. It was clear to Katie that the three of them had to become a team and that, as the classroom teacher, she needed to take on the leadership role in deciding how to deal with their new student. She had never supervised a full-time teacher aide, and in the case of Mandy Ward this in itself might be a challenge. Katie also knew that it would be helpful to alter somewhat her relationship with her special education colleague. To do this, it was important that she become as knowledgeable as possible in how to deal with a student with autism. Perhaps even more important, she was certain that she needed to assert herself more than she had up to this point in the year. Although Katie was apprehensive about the future of her class, she was determined to make the most of her challenging situation.

DISCUSSION QUESTIONS:

1. Have you had any experience related to individuals with autism? If so, what observations would you make concerning the individuals you have known or have observed?
2. Describe what you feel is an appropriate relationship between a classroom teacher and a special education consultant who works regularly in the teacher's classroom.
3. What should be the relationship of a teacher to an aide assigned to that teacher's classroom? What specific duties can be performed by a teacher aide? What are some tasks that should be the responsibility of the classroom teacher?
4. What additional steps should Katie take as she prepares for her new student?
5. What should she tell her current class about the new student who will be joining them?

NOTES

1. R. Weiss, "1 in 150 Children in U.S. Has Autism, New Survey Finds," *Washington Post*, February 9, 2007, www.washingtonpost.com/wp-dyn/content/article/2007/02/08 (accessed October 28, 2008).

2. "Autism," *eMedicineHealth*, 2008, www.emedicinehealth.com/autism/page2_em.htm (accessed October 28, 2008).

3. "Autism," *eMedicineHealth*.

4. "Autism Spectrum Disorders Health Center," *WebMD*, May 9, 2008, www.webmd.com/brain/autism/autism-symptoms (accessed October 28, 2008).

5. "Autism Spectrum Disorders Health Center," *WebMD*.

6. "Autism and Your Child," *Family Doctor*, 2008, familydoctor.org/online/famdocen/home/children/parents/special/commons/638.html (accessed October 28, 2008).

7. "What Is Autism?" *Autism Speaks*, www.autsimspeaks.org/whatisit/faq.php (accessed November 29, 2008).

8. "Autism," *eMedicineHealth*.

9. "Autism," *eMedicineHealth*.

10. "Autism," *Health Encyclopedia, a Health Scout Source of USA Today*, 2008, www. healthscout.com/ency/68/317/main.html (accessed October 28, 2008).

11. "Autism," *Health Encyclopedia*.

ADDITIONAL RESOURCES

Cook, B., and M. Semmel. "Peer Acceptance of Included Students with Disabilities as a Function of Severity of Disability and Classroom Composition." *The Journal of Special Education* 33, no. 1 (March 1999): 50–61. Retrieved December 8, 2008, doi:10.1177/002246699903300105.

Hart, J., and K. Whalon. "Promote Academic Engagement and Communication of Students with Autism Spectrum Disorder in Inclusive Settings." *Intervention in School & Clinic* 44, no. 2 (2008, November): 116–20. Retrieved December 8, 2008, from Professional Development Collection database.

Tomasik, M. "Effective Inclusion Activities for High School Students with Multiple Disabilities." *Journal of Visual Impairment & Blindness* 101, no. 10 (October 2007): 657–9. Retrieved December 8, 2008, from PsycINFO database.

Wilson, G. "Be an Active Co-Teacher." *Intervention in School & Clinic* 43, no. 4 (March 2008): 240–43. Retrieved December 8, 2008, from Professional Development Collection database.

Educating Gifted Students

The Future of Gifted and Talented Programs

Unlike the heavily funded mandates for educating students designated as in need of special education, there are few mandates and little state or federal funding for programs for gifted and talented students. Such programs are most often optional, and they are paid for primarily with local funding. The result has often been that wealthy suburban communities are most likely to have such opportunities for their students. While in high schools the number of advanced placement classes is growing, in most districts special pull-out programs for gifted students at the elementary level are less likely to be found in poorer districts. The *New York Times* in November 2008 published an article titled "Education for the Gifted, Seen as a Luxury, Faces Cutbacks." The story began with the following sentence: "As financially pressed school districts in the region struggle with declining Federal and State aid, rebellious taxpayers and rising costs, special programs for gifted and talented students are being trimmed, gutted, or eliminated."[1]

Another factor that some critics feel is affecting such programs is the emphasis of the No Child Left Behind law on ensuring that all students pass the required tests in language arts, math, and science. Some observers have claimed that teachers are spending much of their time and energy on the students who with extra help might pass the test. In doing so it has been suggested that children who have no chance of passing and the gifted students are receiving less attention.[2]

Because of budget cuts, teachers who might have had the help of specialists in the field of gifted and talented education may now be solely

responsible for challenging these children. At the same time these teachers
are also dealing with an increasing number of special education students in
their inclusive classrooms. This too can make meeting the needs of gifted
students more difficult.

Betty Kennedy had been the gifted and talented teacher at the Dewitt Clinton Elementary School for the previous fourteen years. During this time she had been responsible for an extremely successful pull-out program for gifted children in grades 1–6. At each grade level approximately twelve students were identified as those who could most benefit from experiences that would challenge them academically. All of these children had to be two years above grade level in reading and math and, along with their test scores, they needed teacher recommendations for the program. Their IQs were also taken into account as a factor in determining which students would be accepted. Even for those who qualified academically, the program was optional. Because of Mrs. Kennedy's reputation as a creative and fun teacher, almost all of the eligible students seemed eager to participate. The parents of the district were usually very happy when their children were chosen for her classes.

At each of the grade levels the students would report to Mrs. Kennedy's classroom twice each week. The room itself was exciting for the children. Not only did it have an extensive classroom library and a dozen laptop computers, but it featured posters, artwork, and an ever-changing variety of materials that were to be used in her lessons. The students spent most of their time doing projects in science and social studies. Frequently the activities saw the children working in the community with public officials or other individuals in a variety of occupations. The sixth-grade students always participated in the international program known as Odyssey of the Mind. Each year an intellectual problem was offered to students from schools all over the world. The members of her class had several times been successful in local competitions and went on to compete at the state level. In all of her classes she had a way of coming up with new and creative ideas every year. Betty saw her work with these students as very important and she cared deeply about each of them.

Many years earlier she had begun her career as a third-grade teacher and had decided to earn her master's degree in the field of gifted and talented education. Along with teaching at the Dewitt Clinton Elementary School, she had become an active member in the state organization of the Teachers of the Gifted and Talented. Two years previously she had been president of this group. It had been a shock to the faculty and staff the previous May when she announced her retirement.

As a result of an ongoing recession in the local economy, the board of education the previous spring had made a number of staff reductions for the coming year. Along with Betty Kennedy, six other teachers had either announced their retirement or that they would be leaving the district. In the case of five of the seven potential vacancies, the board decided not to fill the positions of those teachers who were leaving. Despite the fact that there had been significant support for the continuation of the gifted and talented program, the board had voted four to three to terminate the program. Betty and other members of the elementary school faculty were devastated by the decision and prepared a petition that sought to overturn the board's action. At the next meeting the same four board members voted and reaffirmed their decision.

Daniel Bush was one of those who was disappointed with the decision to end the gifted and talented program. In his third year as a fourth-grade teacher in the district, he had seen how excited the students who were chosen for the program were both before and after they went to Mrs. Kennedy's class. The students had frequently shared with him information about what they were doing with Mrs. Kennedy. It was only the third week of the new year, but he was already missing the program.

Two of his students, who had been part of Mrs. Kennedy's class the previous year, had also shared with him the fact that they wished she was still here. Mitchell Smith was one of these students, and it seemed obvious that he needed some sort of academic outlet; he was frequently restless during many of Daniel's lessons. This was especially true in math class, where the boy already knew most of what was being taught. What he did not know he learned much more quickly than the rest of the class. As a result, he frequently appeared to be bored and sometimes inattentive. Daniel had been forced several times to ask the boy to pay attention. The possibility that Mitchell would, in time, become a discipline problem had already crossed Daniel's mind. Unless it was possible to find a way to better engage him, there certainly was the possibility of future problems.

Kaylee Heath would never be a discipline problem, but too often she appeared to be in a world all her own. If given the choice, Kaylee would have been happy to sit in the corner and read. Whenever possible she was always reading one of her favorite books. Currently she was engrossed in reading all of the Harry Potter books. She was often uninterested in most of the fourth-grade reading material.

While he was beginning to worry about Mitchell and Kaylee, Daniel was also concerned with three other students that had been placed in his class this year. One boy had been diagnosed with attention deficit hyperactivity disorder and even though he was currently taking Ritalin, there were times when he could be a challenge. There were two other students with learning disabilities who each had individualized education programs that required alternative lessons in certain subjects. At least with these students he had the help of a part-time special education consultant, but with his two gifted children he was very much on his own.

Daniel decided to do some reading to help him better understand the challenge he faced with Mitchell and Kaylee. He first learned that even defining giftedness was somewhat controversial. He had copied out the following quotation from one of his college textbooks:

> To some, the traditional definition of giftedness includes those with an IQ of 130 or higher; to others, the label giftedness is reserved for those with an IQ score of 160 or higher. The National Association for Gifted Children defines five elements of giftedness: artistic and creative talents, intellectual and academic abilities, and leadership skills.[3]

After checking their records Daniel found that, at least in terms of their IQ, both of the children in his class would be considered gifted.

Another source talked about some of the negative possibilities if gifted students were not properly challenged in school.

> Instead of thriving in school, they drop out. The picture is especially dismal for females, children of color, and English language learners who are identified as gifted, and once identified, are more likely to drop out than gifted white males. The result is that many of our nation's brightest and most competent students are lost to neglect and apathy, and some of our most talented youth have not always succeeded at school.
>
> Research shows that a significant number of gifted students contemplate suicide. Gifted students may be haunted by a sense of isolation and loneliness, pressure to achieve, and fear of failure.[4]

As to how schools should deal with these children, the sources he read seemed to concentrate on accelerated programs. Options such as advanced placement classes were available at the high school level, but acceleration was more difficult for elementary students. At one time children would frequently be allowed to skip a grade. Because of the possible impact socially on children, this approach is rarely used today in elementary schools. More common is the attempt to enrich the curriculums of the gifted children.

This was the purpose of Mrs. Kennedy's pull-out program. There was no question that it had been a wonderful example of this type of opportunity for students. It appeared now that enrichment experiences, at least at De-witt Clinton Elementary School, would have to be offered by the classroom teacher. In the cases of Mitchell and Kaylee, that meant that Daniel should be seeking to do something to challenge these children.

With this in mind, he decided to call Betty. There was little question that she would have some suggestions. It also occurred to him that other teachers in the building might be facing similar challenges in their classrooms. Although he was not particularly fond of faculty meetings, he wondered if this was a topic that should be discussed by the teachers who had gifted and talented students in their classes.

DISCUSSION QUESTIONS

1. What suggestions do you have for elementary schools that currently lack a specific program for gifted and talented students?
2. Choosing the grade level and the subject of your choice, describe a lesson or project you could use for one or more gifted students in your classroom.
3. Should special educational programs for gifted and talented students be a major priority for American education? Why? Why not? Should funding for these programs be equal to the money that is now allowed for learning disabled students?

NOTES

1. J. Nordheimer, "Education for the Gifted, Seen as a Luxury, Faces Cutbacks," *New York Times*, November 29, 1992, query.nytimes.com/gst/fullpage.html?res=9F0C E3D61730F93AA15752C1A9658 (accessed November 3, 2008).

2. D. Viadero, "Study: Low, High Fliers Gain Less under NCLB," *Education Week*, August 1, 2007, 7.

3. D. M. Sadker, M. P. Sadker, and K. R. Zittleman, *Teachers, Schools, and Society* (Boston: McGraw-Hill, 2008), 50.

4. J. Galbraith, "Gifted Youth and Self-Concept," *Gifted Education* 15, no. 2 (May 1989): 15–17.

ADDITIONAL RESOURCES

Bracey, G. "Performance at the Top." *Phi Delta Kappan* 90, no. 1 (September 2008): 71–72. Retrieved December 8, 2008, from Professional Development Collection database.

Kaplan, S. "Projects: Yay or Nay." *Gifted Child Today* (Spring 2008): 47–65. Retrieved December 8, 2008, from Professional Development Collection database.

McAllister, B., and L. Plourde. "Enrichment Curriculum: Essential For Mathematically Gifted Students." *Education* 129, no. 1 (Fall 2008): 40–49. Retrieved December 8, 2008, from Professional Development Collection database.

Phillips, S. "Are We Holding Back Our Students That Possess the Potential to Excel?" *Education* 129, no. 1 (Fall 2008): 50–55. Retrieved December 8, 2008, from Professional Development Collection database.

We Can't Keep Losing So Many Kids

How Can We Stop Students from Dropping Out of School?

There is no question that the school dropout rate in the United States is a national problem. Although controversy has been continuing over the best and fairest way to measure the number of dropouts, it is clear that far too many of our students fail to graduate from high school. These young people not only create a problem for themselves but also negatively impact society as a whole. They are "much more likely than their peers who graduate to be unemployed, living in poverty, receiving public assistance, in prison, unhealthy . . . and ultimately single parents with children who drop out of high school themselves."[1]

While the good news is that more students are going to college than ever, "the number of students failing to complete high school is rising. Nationally the high school graduation rate hovers at around seventy percent. In many cities, both large and small, the rate is closer to fifty percent."[2]

The economic implications for those who drop out of school are especially sobering. Recent census figures show the stark differences in average income statistics. For those with a bachelor's degree, the average income is listed as $51,554; those with a high school education earn an average of $28,645, while the average income of a dropout is $19,169.[3] When considering dropout rates, it is clear that significantly more minority students, students from low-income families, and disabled students are included among those who leave school early.

For teachers of secondary students, especially those working in our cities, the above statistics cannot help but bring to mind specific young people who have left school early. Often these students are, for teachers, a living and painful symbol of the failure of our schools.

The dropout rate at West Side High School was very much on Greg Madison's mind as this school year was ending. During the last week of classes before exam week, he had had conversations with two students that he could not forget. As a first-year math teacher in one of the five high schools in the city of Greenville, he had not thought very much about dropouts in the past. While several of the ninth-grade students he had had during his first year of teaching had stopped attending school during the year, he had never really talked with them before they left. His first conversation this week was with one of his favorite students, Michael Jones.

The boy had stopped by his classroom after school to say good-bye. He informed Greg that in August he would be sixteen years old and that he would not be returning to school in September. The boy's news was a total shock to Greg. Michael had been a solid math student all year. If it had not been for his erratic attendance, he might have been an honor student. When he did come to class, it was obvious that he learned new mathematical concepts easily and that he could actually help some of his friends with the practice problems. When Greg asked why Michael was considering quitting school, the boy seemed reticent to talk about his reasons.

When Greg told him that he was a bright young man, Michael responded by saying, "Tell that to Mr. Lawrence and Mrs. Wilson." These two individuals were his English and social studies teachers. Michael told him that these teachers "don't like the way I read and talk. When I write a paper there are red marks all over it. They always say that I use 'improper grammar' and 'sentence structure,' whatever that means." The boy went on to say that "I just write the way I talk. For them it's like I'm 'speaking another language.'"

Michael went on to note that he had failed fifth grade and was already a year behind. If he failed social studies and English this year, it would mean he would be in the ninth grade for another year. If that happened, he was sure he would be at least twenty years old before he graduated, if he ever graduated. In addition, he told Greg that he knew he could get a job at McDonald's and that the extra money would help out his mom with her bills.

Greg knew that Michael was from a single-parent home, and he remembered meeting Mrs. Jones at the parent open house earlier in the year. She had been extremely happy to hear that her son was a fine math student. After meeting her, Greg was sure that the boy's mother would not want him to quit school. When he asked Michael about his mom's reaction to the decision to leave school, he was told that she had said that he would be "exactly like me, and you will never get a good job." Whatever his mom's reaction, it had not changed Michael's mind. When pushed for any other reasons for dropping out, he admitted that he "didn't really like school." It made Greg feel a bit better when the boy said that "your class ain't so bad, and sometimes I like science when we really do something, but most of the time I am bored and feel that nobody cares if I'm here or not."

Greg tried to reassure Michael that his teachers really did care, but the boy responded that "they have a funny way of showing it." Before he left the classroom, Greg managed to say that he would be in touch. There was little response to his parting statement, and Greg was fairly sure that Michael did not expect to hear from him again.

As if this conversation was not disturbing enough, the next day after school he was visited by another of his students, Anita McCoy. A very quiet girl, Anita was an average math student, the type whom it was easy to take for granted. She was in school every day and always did her homework, but it was clear to Greg that math was not her favorite subject. A faculty-room conversation with her English teacher a few months ago had surprised him when he learned that Anita was a very talented writer. She had written several poems, one of which had been printed in the school newspaper. The English teacher had told Greg that she had also written two very interesting short stories.

During his after-school conversation with Anita, he learned that she too was not planning to return to school next year. When asked why, she reported that she was pregnant. Taken aback by this news, he responded by assuring his student that she could come back to school after she had her baby. He had already known several students who had continued in school while they were pregnant and returned to classes a few weeks after the baby was born. He decided not to ask her about the father of the baby, but rather inquired whether or not there was a family member who could care for the child while she was in school. Anita said that this was impossible because both her grandmother and mother had to work. In any case, she said, "I believe it is my responsibility."

At the end of this conversation it seemed that this potentially talented young lady would also become a high school dropout. The only advice he could think of for her was to talk to her guidance counselor. She was quick to respond by saying, "What can she do?"

That Friday evening after dinner, Greg told his wife Anna about his conversations. After hearing his story she said, "We can't keep losing so many kids." She was sincerely bothered by the stories of Greg's two students and suggested that there must be schools with specific programs to keep kids like Michael and Anita in school. With this possibility in mind he spent the next hour on the computer to learn as much as he could about the dropout problem.

One helpful article that he read included some interesting information about dropouts.

- The relationships between students and teachers are the most important factor in a student's school experience, whether positive or negative.
- The disruptiveness of peers in school causes students to feel distracted and unsafe, leading to an increased chance of dropping out.
- The pace of instruction is an important reason youth give for leaving school—students who need extra attention and don't receive it are likely to drop out.
- Personal problems cause youths to leave school if they do not have a trusted adult from whom they can seek help.
- Students in small alternative programs appreciate the increased attention and the opportunity to work at their own pace.
- Weak academic skills can cripple efforts to recover dropouts in "second-chance" programs unless they receive even more attention from community volunteers.
- Economic needs can compete with pursuing education after dropping out.
- Students who come from single-parent families, have a mother who dropped out of high school, have parents who provide low support for learning, or have parents who do not know their friends' parents well, are also all at a higher risk of dropping out than other students.[4]

Another survey of five hundred dropouts included the percentages of students citing different reasons for leaving school.

- 47 percent said classes were not interesting.
- 43 percent missed too many days to catch up.

* 45 percent entered high school poorly prepared by their earlier schooling.
* 69 percent said they were not motivated to work hard.
* 35 percent said they were failing.
* 32 percent said they left to get a job.
* 25 percent left to become parents.
* 22 percent left to take care of a relative.[5]

He also copied some programs that schools were trying to help deal with the problem. They included

* evening classes
* more GED opportunities
* tutoring
* allowing students to return when older[6]

An additional survey showed that former dropouts believe the following approaches would help to deal with the problem.

* Improve teaching and curricula to enhance the connection between school and work. Eighty-one percent of dropouts said there should be more opportunities for "real-world" learning so that students can see the connection between school and getting a job.
* Improve access to support struggling students. Eighty-one percent of dropouts surveyed wanted "better" teachers. Seventy-five percent wanted smaller classes. Sixty percent believed that more tutoring, summer school, and extra time with teachers would have improved their chances of graduating.
* Foster academics. Seventy percent of dropouts said that "increasing supervision in school" and 62 percent said "more classroom discipline" was necessary to ensure success. Fifty-seven percent said that their schools "did not do enough" to help students feel safe from violence.
* Promote close relationships with adults. Only 41 percent of dropouts reported having someone to talk to about personal problems. Sixty-two percent said they would like to see schools do more to help students with problems outside of class. Only 47 percent said the schools even bothered to contact them after they dropped out.[7]

The last article he read was one from the *Seattle Times*. It included the fact that a considerable amount of grant money was available for dropout prevention programs. The newspaper story noted that the most important initiatives were being financed by the Bill and Melinda Gates Foundation, which was seeking "to double the number of low-income students who complete some kind of college or post–high school degree." During the past eight years the foundation has spent $4 billion; half on scholarships and half on its work to improve our nation's high schools.[8]

It occurred to Greg that there must be schools that are trying to do something about the number of students they are losing, but he was unaware of anything specific his district was attempting. Even though he was a mere first-year teacher, it occurred to him that he might become a catalyst for doing something for students like Michael and Anita.

DISCUSSION QUESTIONS

1. What, if anything, can Greg do to help his two students?
2. In your opinion, what are some possible initiatives a district might try to reduce its dropout rate?
3. As a teacher, what can you do with your students and within your school to try to keep potential dropouts from leaving?

NOTES

1. R. Glass and M. Rose, "Tune Out Turn Off Drop Out," *American Teacher*, November 2008, 8.

2. "Tune Out Turn Off Drop Out," 8.

3. B. Pytel, "Dropouts Give Reasons," Suite 101.com, November 4, 2006, educationalissues.suite101.com/article.cfm/dropouts_give_reasons (accessed November 14, 2008).

4. "Dropout Prevention," Solutions for America, 2003, solutionsforamerica.org/healthyfam/dropout_prevention.html (accessed November 14, 2008).

5. "Dropouts Give Reasons."

6. "Dropouts Give Reasons."

7. "Dropout Prevention."

8. L. Shaw, "Gates Foundation Releases Ambitious New Giving Plans for Education," *Seattle Times*, November 11, 2008, seattletimes.nwsource.com/html/ localnews/2008378857_webgateseducaion11m.html (accessed November 14, 2008).

ADDITIONAL RESOURCES

"High School Dropouts Cost US $319B over Lifetime." *Education Week* (April 2, 2009). www.edweek.org/ew/articles/2009/04/02/259925ghighschooldropouts_ap.ht ml?tkn=PWYCyBarxN9%2FLgug7IbWQVr%2FYPX%2BX1qMKlmM.

Kingsbury, K. "No Dropouts Left Behind: New Rules on Grad Rates." *Time* (October 30, 2008). www.time.com/time/nation/article/0,8599,1854758,00.html?iid=sphere-inline-bottom.

Suh, R. "School Dropout Issues" (pp. 1-1). Great Neck Publishing (2008). Retrieved December 8, 2008, from Research Starters–Education database.

Do We Really Have to Bribe Them?

Using Financial Incentives to Motivate Students

School districts throughout the nation are using or considering using incentive programs to motivate their students. A single grant funded by Exxon/Mobil has created programs in seven states. The money is being used to pay students $100 for receiving a passing grade on any advanced placement test. In New York City the reward for students in grades 4–7 for improving their test scores in English and math is $500. A suburban district outside of Atlanta, Georgia, has decided on another approach; it is now paying students in grades 8–11 for attending a fifteen-week "Learn & Earn" class after school. With the national minimum wage currently set at $5.85 an hour, the students participating in this program are paid $8 an hour. There are other unique ideas being tried in Baltimore, Maryland, and in Texas. Perhaps one of the oldest plans is one in Dallas, Texas, which was begun during the 1995–1996 school year.[1]

Large school districts are not the only ones becoming involved in this growing practice. Often the initiative for these experiments originates with those outside the school community. It can be an individual or a group that makes the proposal. In the future it is quite possible that even more districts will consider this option for improving academic results. While some are enthusiastic about using cash or gifts to encourage students, there are also many serious critics of the idea.

The possibility came up in a conversation at the coffee hour after church. Clark Richards, president of the Madison City School District Teachers Union, was about ready to try to gather his wife and head home to be sure he would not miss the kickoff of the early National Football League game. He was approached by Larry Tompkins, the chief executive officer of the local food processing plant. Larry was a respected leader, both in the church and in the community. It was rumored that after founding and managing Tompkins Foods for the past three decades, he was preparing to retire. He had already cut back his hours at the plant and his son Scott was the heir apparent. Clark and Larry had known each other for several years, as they were members of the local gym and worked out at the same time on most weekdays.

Larry began the conversation by saying that he was looking for some positive ways to make a difference. He was thinking about a plan that would allow him to give something back to the community that had been so good to him and his family. An article in the *Washington Post* had led him to consider an idea he was obviously excited about. As justification for the idea, he quoted the mayor of Chicago, Richard M. Daley, who had said, "Wealthy parents in the suburban area, they give their kids a car. They take them on a trip to Hawaii. They send them around the world." Talking about most of the students in Chicago, the mayor had argued, "These kids don't even get out of their homes for many, many years."[2] This article caused Larry to think about a possible academic incentive program for Madison High School.

Larry went on to share the fact that he had certainly offered incentives to his son when he was going through school and he couldn't help asking himself why kids from less affluent homes should not be rewarded for good grades. He said that "incentives worked well for Scott, and he got into an Ivy League school. Before long, he'll be running a company with 450 employees. I remember offering him the possibility of taking flying lessons if he made the honor roll every quarter. He did it, and now he flies his own private plane. I also doubled his allowance every time he made the honor roll."

It was obvious to Clark that his friend was very enthusiastic about giving some money to the school district to reward students for academic success. Larry had even thought about an amount to kick off the program. He said he was willing to donate $10,000 the first year for students and allow the district to use the money in any way the board felt was appropriate. Based on reading the *Post* article, which suggested that incentives worked best when both the students and teachers were rewarded, he said he was willing to donate an additional $10,000 to be given to teachers whose students were successful. Just as with the students, Larry was willing to leave the details of such a reward system for the teachers to the school district. Even more encouraging was his assurance that if the plan were successful, he and his company would undoubtedly be willing to fund the initiative at an even higher level in the future.

Clark found it difficult to react to this very generous offer, but he did promise to talk with some teachers and administrators and get back to Larry by next Sunday. During the week after this conversation, Clark began to read about various student incentive programs. He started with the article that had prompted Larry to consider such a program and was surprised at how much of that story was devoted to critics of incentive plans for students. One paragraph had stood out in his mind, and he had copied it out of the paper. It read,

> Critics denounce the initiatives as bribery and say the money could be better invested into ideas known to work, such as smaller class size. They also point to a body of psychological research suggesting that tangible rewards can erode children's intrinsic motivation. DePaul University education professor Ronald Chennault says there are ethical issues posed by the ventures, most of which are experimental and dependent on private funding and local support. "The potential for harm is, what happens after the incentive no longer exists?" Chennault asks. "Not everything is worth trying."[3]

The article also referenced what it called the "inconclusive research" that has been done concerning the success of incentive programs. One thing seemed clear, and it was that a commitment by adults was needed for such programs if they were to be successful. This fact seemed to support using money to reward teachers as well as students. The bottom line seemed to be expressed by a researcher who concluded that these programs were "not a silver bullet . . . but it's better than sitting around and doing nothing."[4]

After reading this and other articles about the subject, Clark was far from fully convinced that these programs were the best way to improve student achievement. It even occurred to him that he might try to convince Larry to start a preschool program or to use the money to reduce class sizes in the district. Unfortunately, at least at the level he was now thinking, there would not be enough money to finance either of these options. In any case he knew he had committed himself to some conversations concerning the proposal. It seemed most appropriate to begin with Kym Woodard, the superintendent of schools in the district. After describing the offer to the superintendent, he was not altogether surprised that she was not willing to take a position on the proposal. Kym did tell him that she would discuss the matter with some board members and get back to him later in the week.

She had done so on Thursday evening and told Clark that the board members had reacted in a variety of ways. Two of them objected to the idea of paying students for doing what they should be doing without having to be bribed. Even though there was opposition, the superintendent told Clark it appeared that a majority would favor continuing discussions on the possibility of moving forward on the project. Two members of the board were definitely enthusiastic about the idea. Although the superintendent herself appeared to be far from enthusiastic, she said that it would probably be a good idea to invite Mr. Tompkins to a future board meeting. Clark had told the superintendent he would be meeting with the executive committee of the teachers union on Friday after school and that he would let her know about the reaction of the teachers in the group.

To say that the executive committee meeting was lively would be an understatement. Despite the fact that it was a Friday afternoon, the group had come alive. Nancy Compise, a veteran English teacher, had been the first to react, saying that she didn't need to pay her students for doing their work. For her, a good teacher or parent could motivate students without paying them off. Clark secretly felt some sympathy for this point of view. Although he and his wife might have occasionally rewarded their three children for good grades, it had not been necessary to pay them for doing well in school. While he didn't share his own feelings with the group, several others had reservations about a student incentive plan. One of the officers of the group said that Larry would be better off using the money to give scholarships to worthy students.

Just as with the board of education, there were also those who liked the idea. The treasurer of the union, who was a seventh-grade math teacher, believed some of his students would be motivated by the possibility of a cash reward. He claimed that "for some of these kids, fifty dollars is a fortune. If it got them to do their homework it would be worth it." Another member of the group was encouraged by the idea of financial rewards for teachers. He admitted that "I could use a few extra bucks. Maybe I would not have to paint so many houses this summer."

By the time the meeting ended, Clark was not sure whether a majority of his committee was in favor of the plan. It was possible that had a vote been taken, he might have had to cast the deciding ballot. As a result, he decided to not even call for a vote. When he shared the results of the meeting with the superintendent, Kym only said, "I guess unless the teachers would fail to support such a plan, we should at least pursue it."

Clark knew that on Sunday morning he would be asked again about the proposal. In his own mind he was still unsure and even thought about staying home from church, but knew that he would have to react sometime. In doing so he couldn't help but remember the question raised by one of his fellow teachers during the meeting: "Do we really have to bribe them?"

DISCUSSION QUESTIONS:

1. Do you like the idea of cash or gift incentives for students? Why? Why not?
2. What should Clark say to Larry about the proposal?
3. What do you think would happen in a district that faced this type of situation?

NOTES

1. G. Toppo, "Good Grades Pay Off Literally," *USA Today*, August 1, 2008, www.usatoday.com/news/education/2008-01-27-grades_N.htm (accessed November 18, 2008).

2. B. Turque, "When a Gold Star Is Not Enough," *Washington Post*, November 10, 2008, 35.

3. "When a Gold Star Is Not Enough."

4. "When a Gold Star Is Not Enough."

ADDITIONAL RESOURCES

"A Paying Job for Kids: Test Taking." *American School Board Journal* (April 2008). Retrieved December 15, 2008, from Professional Development Collection database.

"City Will Reward Students with Phones." *New York Sun* (February 28, 2008). www.nysun.com/new-york/city-will-reward-students-with-phones/72038.

"No Child Left Behind Summer Reading Achievers Program Provides Free Books to Atlanta Students." *No Child Left Behind Extra Credit* (May 15, 2003). Retrieved December 15, 2008, from PsycEXTRA database.

He Hasn't Helped Me at All

The Importance of
Teacher Mentor Programs

"It is commonly known that 50% of new teachers leave the profession within the first five years of teaching."[1] As a result of this unfortunate statistic, since the early 1980s, school districts and state governments have sought ways to improve how schools deal with their new faculty members. One important development is teacher mentor programs. Typical of this initiative is a mandatory program for first-year teachers in the state of New York. The key provisions of the state plan are as follows:

- The purpose of the mentoring experience is to improve the skill and retention of new teachers as they transition from academic preparation to their first professional appointment.

- The mentoring program must be developed consistent with Article XIV of the Civil Service Law. Any mentoring program components that fall within the purview of contractual negotiations should be addressed accordingly.

- The mentor's role is one of guidance and support. However, the mentor may have an evaluative role as well as guidance and support, if this stipulation has been negotiated and agreed upon in the local teachers' contract. If the mentor's role is solely that of guidance and support, information emerging from mentoring activities and the mentoring relationship is confidential.

- Required elements of the mentoring program include
  - A mentor selection procedure—published and available to district staff and the public upon request
  - Mentor training and preparation
  - Defined set of mentor activities
  - Allocation of time for mentoring activities to take place
  - The district must maintain documentation of mentoring activities. Items to be recorded: names and teacher certificate numbers of mentors and teachers served, type of mentoring activities, and the number of clock hours of mentoring provided to each new teacher.[2]

The policy goes on to discuss the overall induction process for new teachers. Along with mentoring, the term *induction* refers to what some would call the orientation of new teachers to a school district. This process usually begins with meetings specifically designed for new teachers and goes on to provide an ongoing professional growth process for those beginning their careers in the district. The New York policy also argues that "teacher induction has consistently shown to be effective in stemming teacher attrition. Further, teacher mentoring appears to significantly impact a beginning teacher's movement along the continuum of skill development and self-confidence as a teacher."[3] Whether programs are state mandated or voluntarily created by individual districts, some are much more successful than others.

Charlie Sherwin and Martin Carpenter were both first-year high school teachers. After graduating the previous May, Charlie had taken a social studies teaching position and Martin had been hired to teach math in a neighboring high school but had not had the opportunity to talk in great detail about the first four months of their first teaching experience. As they were riding together back to their college to watch a basketball game, their conversation turned to their faculty mentors. What they quickly found out was that school districts varied, especially in regard to their teacher mentor programs.

Beginning with the time devoted to orienting newly hired teachers, the friends discussed what had happened to them thus far in the school year. Charlie mentioned that he had two days of teacher orientation. "The first day was for the new teachers in all of the schools in the district. We met in the district office and met all of the central office personnel." He went on to talk about the superintendent spending the entire morning with the group and describing in detail the community and some history of the school district. His message had concluded with a PowerPoint presentation on the goals of the district. Charlie also remembered that the president of the teachers union had spoken to the group and distributed copies of the teacher contract.

He went on to describe the great lunch and the bus trip that the group took that first afternoon. One of the history teachers, a lifelong resident of the district, acted as a guide on the bus and talked about various points of interest in the community. Charlie told his friend that he had seen some very affluent neighborhoods, but also there had been two rather large mobile home parks and a section of the district that had "obviously seen better days." Martin responded with, "It sounds like fun and probably very helpful. What did you do the second day?"

Charlie reported that all of the teachers had gone to their individual schools, and when they arrived, "we had coffee and the most delicious danishes that I've ever tasted." He noted that there were five new teachers at the high school. First they had met with the principal, Mrs. Harris, who distributed and explained the highlights in the policy handbook. She then went on to introduce the two assistant principals, who talked about the school's discipline policies. This was followed by brief comments from a member of the guidance staff, the school psychologist, and the school social worker.

"After another great lunch the director of the mentor program told us that we would be meeting our individual mentors that afternoon. During his comments he mentioned that we would be meeting twice a month as a group to learn and to share our problems and experiences." Charlie said that perhaps the best part of the two days was the second afternoon when he went to his classroom, where he met and talked to the man assigned as his mentor. He told Martin that during the afternoon they had discussed getting the room ready and what should happen on the first day of school. "He gave me a bunch of helpful suggestions on how I might get off to a good start on the first day."

After hearing about Charlie's experience, Martin asked, "Do you want to hear about my so-called orientation? Our half-day meeting was at the high school. All eleven of the new teachers in the high school arrived early, and the school secretary did not know where we should go." He went on to relate that "about two minutes before the meeting was scheduled to start, our principal arrived and took us all down to the school library, where the librarian and her aides were shelving books. Because of the way the tables were arranged, we were spread all over the room. At times it was hard to even hear what the principal was saying." Martin could not help but portray the principal's remarks as being less than informative or helpful. He shared the fact that "all I remember is that he said that we were 'the cream of the crop' and he told us how lucky we were to be chosen to work in 'our fine school.' Although many of us had had a building tour when we came for the interview, he gave us a quick tour and then said he knew we wanted to spend time in our classrooms, and he briefly mentioned that we would meet our mentors next week. The principal ended the meeting by telling us we could stay in the building as long as we wished and that there was coffee available in the faculty room." Charlie could not help but ask his friend, "And that was it?" Martin told him that he had gone to his classroom and tried to write a lesson plan and arrange the room for the first day of classes. He had left school at 1:00 because he was hungry.

When asked about his mentor, Martin replied that "he hasn't helped me at all." Martin shared the fact that his mentor, Rick Kirnan, had told him that he had been assigned the job and that "as far as I know, he has had little or no training as to what he's supposed to do as a mentor. At our first meeting, he as much as told me that he was not sure of his exact role but that he would do what he could." Charlie was surprised to learn that Martin's mentor was a Spanish teacher who knew very little about teaching math, which was his friend's department.

Martin went on to explain that "when I have asked him a question, I am not sure he even listens well enough to understand my problem. When he does, his answer goes on and on about how he does things in his Spanish class." Another concern Martin expressed was that he was unsure whether his mentor could be trusted to keep their conversations confidential. He related how on one occasion, when his mentor had no idea how to answer a question, Rick had responded with, "I need to ask my wife." Martin explained that "the problem with that is, he is married to the secretary of the assistant principal." He went on to explain that the last thing he wanted was for an administrator to know about every problem he had.

It was obvious to Charlie that his friend was having a hard time with his mentor. Martin's final comment concerning Rick was that "I hardly ever see him, and that is all right with me. The only advice he has given me so far has been to teach my math classes just like he does his Spanish classes. I can't help but think that his solution to every problem is to do it his way."

Charlie hesitated to even talk about his mentor, Evan Williams, who was a fellow social studies teacher with twenty years of experience in the district. Charlie had quickly learned that Evan was a respected member of the faculty and was also well known throughout the community as a master teacher. Unlike Martin's mentor, Evan was a very good listener. He was an active listener who asked probing questions to clarify the topic being discussed. Charlie felt free to share his ideas, as Evan appeared to be very nonjudgmental. He also was certain that their conversations would be kept confidential. Even though his mentor was considerably older than he was, he felt comfortable with him in any situation. Early in the semester he had been invited to Evan's home to have dinner with his family. At the district-wide faculty picnic Evan had made a conscious effort to introduce Charlie to people he had not yet met. In doing so he usually said something complimentary about Charlie. There was no question that, as a new teacher, he felt that he had an advocate with Evan.

As he shared with Martin, he continued to praise Evan for the frequency of their meetings and for all the helpful suggestions and materials he had been given. He also shared his opinion that "unlike your guy, he gives me something to read, or lends me a visual aid to review. In the end it is my decision." The last thing Charlie shared with Martin was the fact that the new teachers were meeting twice a month. At each session there was a chance to raise questions and talk about any problems they might have. In addition, there was a specific discussion topic for each meeting, which he always found helpful. After just a couple of sessions the new teachers developed an openness that helped to make their time together both useful and fun.

When the men reached the college they put their conversation on hold. Over the next few hours they enjoyed the basketball game and talking with a couple of other teacher education graduates who had come back to campus. One of them was very excited about her job, while the other seemed less pleased.

On the ride home, Charlie asked Martin, "How are you feeling about teaching after one semester?" He was not surprised when his friend answered with, "I am not sure that I want to do this the rest of my life." To encourage his friend Charlie assured him that "you are a natural teacher and you can't let yourself become discouraged. It isn't your fault that you have an incompetent principal and mentor. Remember, it's really about the kids." Charlie was not sure about what he had said or whether or not it helped, but he felt bad that Martin's teaching career was beginning so poorly. He, on the other hand, felt that he would not mind doing what he was doing for the next forty years.

DISCUSSION QUESTIONS

1. What sort of orientation or induction program would be most helpful to you when you begin your career in a new school district?
2. What do you see as the important elements in an effective mentoring program in any school district?
3. What qualities do you feel are most important for a mentor?

NOTES

1. "Teacher Retention a Critical National Problem," *National Commission on Teaching and America's Future*, www.nctaf.org/resources/news/weekly_news_digest/April17.htm (accessed November 24, 2008).

2. "Guidelines for Implementing District-Based Teacher Mentoring Programs," *New York State Education Department*, www.highered.nysed.gov/tcert/resteachers/guidemenprog.htm (accessed November 24, 2008).

3. "Guidelines for Implementing District-Based Teacher Mentoring Programs."

ADDITIONAL RESOURCES

Hudson, P. "Examining Mentors' Practices for Enhancing Preservice Teachers' Pedagogical Development in Mathematics and Science." *Mentoring & Tutoring: Partnership in Learning* 15, no. 2 (May 2007): 201–17. Retrieved December 15, 2008, doi:10.1080/13611260601086394.

Mullen, C. "Supporting the Professional Development of New and Seasoned Practitioners." *Mentoring & Tutoring: Partnership in Learning* 15, no. 3 (August 2007): 219–21. Retrieved December 15, 2008, doi:10.1080/13611260701201612.

Wong, H., and R. Wong. "Academic Coaching Produces More Effective Teachers." *Education Digest* 74, no. 1 (September 2008): 59–64. Retrieved December 15, 2008, from Professional Development Collection database.

Zuljan, M., and J. Vogrinc. "A Mentor's Aid in Developing the Competences of Teacher Trainees." *Educational Studies* 33, no. 4 (December 2007): 373–84. Retrieved December 15, 2008, doi:10.1080/03055690701423473.

The Cultural Dilemma

The Challenges of Teaching in an Urban Setting

Despite the civil rights movement over the past half-century in the United States, it can be argued that "today's students are more segregated than they were three decades ago."[1] With the movement of whites to the suburbs during the past half-century, schools located in the cities throughout the United States now find their student bodies made up primarily of nonwhite children. Early attempts at busing and other affirmative action programs have, for the most part, been curtailed by court decisions, and our society has seemingly accepted the racial separation of our children. This racial segregation in our schools is made even more complicated by the fact that teachers in urban schools are primarily middle-class whites who have lived their lives in suburban and rural communities.

Teacher education college programs, which also are often located on campuses in suburban and rural communities, frequently have difficulty providing their students sufficient classroom experience in urban schools. In addition, many of the teacher education faculty themselves have little or no experience working with minority students in city schools. The result of these factors can and often does create a "cultural dilemma" for both students and teachers.

Garrick Brown had been teaching for only three months in the Monroe City School District. He was a graduate of a small rural high school and had earned both his bachelor's and master's degrees from a Christian college in the suburbs. With the exception of spending thirty hours as a student observer in an honors magnet high school in the city, he had never experienced being in an urban school. The time he spent in the high school honors class had been a learning opportunity, and he now looked back at it as a positive experience. In fact, this opportunity had convinced him that he might enjoy teaching in the city.

Even at this rather elite high school, he had been very aware of the poverty of many of his students and of their academic problems. It was his confidence that he could succeed in such a setting, along with some Christian idealism, that caused him to apply for a position in the city of Monroe. On the other hand, despite the fact that he had an excellent grade point average, successful student teaching experiences, and some exceptional references, the only job offer he had received was from the city. When Garrick received the call from the personnel office, he was told that he would be notified of his building assignment by July 1.

He had been hoping to teach at the honors magnet school where he had observed, but this was not to be. When he finally received the letter from the school district, it informed him that he would be teaching ninth-grade English at West High School. The next day he visited the school to meet with the principal. What he found was a sixty-year-old building that was not in the greatest condition. Even more disconcerting was the location of the school. It was a high-poverty area, and he noticed that there were almost no white people.

While he had been at the magnet honors school he had observed a fairly diverse student population. At West High School, this was certainly not the case. In his five classes he had no more than half a dozen white students. The first weeks of school had been extremely difficult for him, but by the end of November he was feeling more comfortable with his students. Unfortunately, a conversation with a number of his ninth graders the previous day had upset him. As an English teacher, Garrick had been working hard trying to convince his students to use what he considered to be Standard English in their written work and during classroom discussions. He would always react and correct them when they used words or expressions that would not have been acceptable in either his own high school or in his college classrooms.

In the exchange he had with the students the previous day one boy had said, "We city cats swear and use language that you don't like. We have a way of talking with each other that you can't seem to accept. Sometimes we act in ways that some of our teachers find offensive, but really, it's just how we act.

We aren't going to change." It was obvious to Garrick that the other students in the group rallied behind the boy's assertion.

That evening, while considering his student's comment, Garrick decided to look back at his *Foundations of Education* textbook, where he remembered reading about something called "the anti-achievement dilemma." When he found the section he was searching for, it talked about a study done in Washington, D.C., at a school that had a 99 percent black population. The study had found that

> the students actively discouraged each other from working to achieve because attaining academic success was seen as "acting white." "Acting white" was understood to include speaking Standard English, listening to white music and radio stations, being on time, studying in the library, working hard, and getting good grades. Students who did well in school were called "brainiacs," a term synonymous with jerk.[2]

What struck him most was the point dealing with "speaking Standard English." He also found the fear of "acting white" to be something he sensed in his students. It was certainly true that, for most of them, it did not seem to be desirable to be thought of as being a "brain." Garrick was so concerned about the issue, and what to do, that he decided to e-mail his favorite education professor to see what he might suggest.

In his message he wrote about his concern that "an adversarial relationship" might be forming between him and his students. Garrick also explained that during their discussion, he had said to the students that "each of us has the power to break the molds we grow up in." It was this comment that had seemed to create tension, and he explained to Dr. Debolt that a student had interpreted his comment as a way of saying that "my way is better than your culture's way." Garrick explained in his e-mail that it had not been his intent to make a value judgment. He ended his message with a cry for help as he asked, "How can I put down the idea that they can break the negative actions of their cultures without having them think I am attacking what they've been taught by the people they love? How can I make them want to change? Should I want them to change? This question has been driving me crazy, so I thought I'd give you a crack at it."

That same evening he received an answer from his professor that read as follows:

Garrick,

Difficult question. In our culture there is a mainstream, educated way of interacting for social, educational, cultural, and business activities. Students need to realize that the subcultural variations may be accepted for social interactions among members of the subculture, but not among the larger culture.

Your discussion is similar to those that surround Ebonics. It might be helpful for you to visit some of that literature.

I am not sure if this helps. It is somewhat like money. If a small group of people accepts walnuts in exchange for services or goods, that works for them. If, however, one of them tries to exchange walnuts for goods with someone from outside of the group and that person does not accept the walnuts, then the transaction breaks down. It is similar with language and other components of culture.

Dr. Debolt

Garrick had gone to bed that evening thinking about the example of money suggested by Dr. Debolt and wondering how it would work with his students. At the same time he knew that his dilemma concerning how to deal with cultural differences would be one he would face as long as he taught in his city school.

DISCUSSION QUESTIONS

1. Do you think that the issues raised in this case study are realistic? Why or why not?

2. What can teacher education programs do to better prepare students who come from suburban and rural areas to teach in urban schools?

3. If Garrick has a follow-up discussion with his students about their language concerns, what should he say?

NOTES

1. D. M. Sadker, M. P. Sadker, and K. R. Zittleman, *Teachers, Schools, and Society* (Boston: McGraw Hill, 2008), 288.

2. Sadker, *Teachers, Schools, and Society*, 288.

ADDITIONAL RESOURCES

Gordon, J. "Inadvertent Complicity: Colorblindness in Teacher Education." *Educational Studies* 38, no. 2 (October 2005): 135–53. Retrieved February 2, 2009, doi:10.1207/s15326993es3802_5.

Hill, K. "A Historical Analysis of Desegregation and Racism in a Racially Polarized Region: Implications for the Historical Construct, a Diversity Problem, and Transforming Teacher Education Toward Culturally Relevant Pedagogy." *Urban Education* 44, no. 1 (January 2009): 106–39. Retrieved February 2, 2009, from Academic Search Premier database.

Spencer, M., E. Noll, J. Stoltzfus, and V. Harpalani. "Identity and School Adjustment: Revisiting the Acting White Assumption." *Educational Psychologist* 36, no. 1 (Winter 2001): 21–30. Retrieved January 28, 2009, from Professional Development Collection database.

What Should the Curriculum Be?

The Appropriate Curriculum for Preschool Programs

Since the beginning of the Head Start program in 1965, preschool programs have become an increasingly significant aspect of education in the United States. Although Head Start was designed to better prepare children from low-income families for kindergarten, programs for three- and four-year-olds have become popular for families at all income levels. The entrance of more mothers into the workforce in recent decades has led to a rapid increase in both public and private preschool programs. The trend has also been influenced by studies that "have noted positive effects when comparing children with access to preschool versus children without access."[1]

A number of authorities, as well as some political candidates, have gone so far as to call for universal pre-kindergarten programs for all children. Others would support at least making such classes a publicly financed option for all children. Critics of this idea refer to studies that seem to show that children from low-income homes benefit greatly from such programs, while many middle-class children who stay home with their parents do just as well without any formal preschool education.

Whether or not our nation adopts a universal program is still an open question. Certainly the support of President Obama and many Democrats in Congress suggests that there will be at least the desire to provide more funds for educating our three- and four-year-olds. Even with the movement gaining momentum, it has been pointed out by Lillian Katz that "disputes concerning curriculum and teaching methods go back a long way in the field of Early Childhood Education."[2] In the age of No Child Left Behind, this issue is still very much with us.

Terry Matthews, the principal of East Banks Elementary School, had just spent two weeks during the summer at a "boot camp" for principals on pre-school education. A former sixth-grade teacher, Terry knew that he had a great deal to learn about the subject and that it was very much on the minds of his superintendent and the board of education. In fact, he had been instructed by the administration to use the coming year to prepare for the introduction of two pre-kindergarten classes in his building. These classes were scheduled to begin the following year. His elementary school was probably chosen for this first venture into early childhood education because East Banks Elementary School currently had several classrooms being used for nonacademic pur-poses. A second reason was that the state government was offering financial grants to districts beginning new public preschool programs.

At his summer workshop Terry had learned about the history of preschool education, and also about the state and federal laws governing such programs. Experts had also talked about numerous philosophical and practical issues surrounding the topic. He left the workshop very much aware that debate was ongoing over what should be happening in these classes.

With a year to prepare, Terry thought he would establish an advisory committee made up of faculty members to help plan the program. He asked the teachers in kindergarten and grades 1–3 to choose one representative at their grade level to serve on the committee. Along with the four teachers, he appointed the school guidance counselor and social worker. Prior to the first meeting, Terry had asked each member to do some research and even pro-vided them with some material he had been given at his summer workshop.

Before he called the group together, Terry hoped that the East Banks Board of Education would decide some of the basic issues related to the program. The biggest questions were how the students would be chosen and how many would be in each class. Many district children were already attending private programs that had been established for a number of years. They were held in church basements and in private homes; one large program met in the local YWCA. In addition, there was one Head Start program that did not come close to ac-commodating all of the children who might be eligible based on their family's income. The district had a significant number of lower-income families who would be eager to take advantage of free public preschool classes.

Both the board members and the administrative team expected that if there was open enrollment for the two classes, there would be far more potential students than the district could accommodate. They had also been exposed to some research arguing that while most students benefited from preschool opportunities, those who made the greatest gains were from disadvantaged households. Debate had already begun on how the district could somehow give an extra advantage to those children coming from poorer homes. Up until now, no one was sure if such a policy would even be legal. A less controversial approach would have a simple random drawing of names to select which children could attend the programs. In any case, this was not Terry's main problem. His major task was to develop the best possible curriculum for the program.

At the first meeting of the advisory committee, Terry raised the question concerning the curriculum for the preschool program. He asked the committee what they saw as the most important objectives. It was clear that gaining a consensus on the emphasis within the curriculum would be difficult. Everyone saw a need to include cognitive skills, including teaching the alphabet and numbers. The teachers representing the first, second, and third grades talked a great deal about the variety of readiness they found in their students. Mrs. Tater, the first-grade representative, mentioned how she had one girl in her class last year who was reading on the third-grade level when she started in the first grade. On the other hand, in the same class, there were half a dozen children who were still struggling to recognize many of the easy sight words. It was her opinion that both the preschool program and the kindergarten classes needed to ensure that every child was "ready to succeed in our first-grade reading program."

Both the second- and third-grade teachers agreed that many students were behind in both reading and math when they entered their classes. Mr. Miller, a third-grade teacher, talked about the pressure that the teachers at his grade level were feeling as a result of the mandatory tests required by the No Child Left Behind law. He went on to complain that "those of us who teach third grade are the first to be judged by our test results. You folks in the lower grades don't have these tests to worry about."

Although his colleagues showed some sympathy, they also pointed out that even though the federal government did not require testing before the third grade, their students had to undergo constant assessment. They too felt some of the pressure caused by standardized tests. It was clear that the first-, second-, and third-grade teacher representatives were hoping that the preschool program would have the primary goal of working with students on their basic skills.

Ellen Patavia, the kindergarten representative, was torn over what the new program should emphasize. Having taught at this grade level for more than thirty years, she had seen a general shift in the expectations for the kindergarten program. She remembered that when she began her career, the classes had done a great deal of singing, playing games, and group activities. Ellen had thought of her class as a transition that helped children socially, as well as academically, for first grade. She remembered that her goals included teaching children to share and to function effectively in a group. There was time for independent play and plenty of physical activity. It was also a time to introduce them to music and art, which were used as vehicles to make children positive about their school experience.

In recent years Ellen had seen her kindergarten classes shift to a more academic emphasis. This meant more traditional teacher-centered lessons, and not only drilling the students on their letters, but also introducing phonics. She could not help but think that neither she nor her students were enjoying kindergarten as much as in the past. When Ellen shared this feeling with the group, it brought the guidance counselor and the social worker into the conversation.

Jeff Spence was the first social worker ever assigned to the East Banks Elementary School. He had brought to the meeting an article written by David Crary, an Associated Press journalist, carrying the headline "Experts Bemoan Loss of Kids' Play Time." Quoting a well-known preschool educator, the article argued that "creative, spontaneous play is both vital and endangered." Kathy Hirsh-Pasek, a Temple University psychologist, was quoted as saying, "Without ample opportunity for forms of play that foster innovation and creative thinking—America's children will be at a disadvantage in the global economy." The article went on to list the reasons that children are having less opportunity to play.[3]

Jeff read the following factors to the committee:

- parental fears about letting children play outside on their own
- schools cutting back on recess time
- more emphasis on organized sports and other structured extracurricular activities
- more time spent by kids watching TV, playing video games, and using cell phones
- more emphasis on improving kids' academic skills[4]

The school guidance counselor, Sharon Thorp, had sent her two children to a Montessori school, and she suggested that at least one of the new preschool classes should follow the Montessori Method. Mr. Miller had joked that Sharon was much too liberal for East Banks Elementary School. Whether it was a Montessori class or not, Sharon believed that the curriculum should be "hands-on" and "experience-based." She argued that "these kids have many years ahead of them to do worksheets."

Terry could not help but think after the meeting that the conversation concerning the appropriate preschool curriculum was a good illustration of what he had once read in an article in the *Educational Leadership* magazine. That evening he went home and found the original copy, in which David J. Ferrero described "the hundred years' war in American education" between traditional and progressive educators. He even copied the author's description of this conflict.

> To oversimplify an already oversimplified dichotomy, progressives incline toward pedagogical approaches that start with student interest and emphasize hands-on engagement with their physical and social environments, whereas traditionalists tend to start with pre-existing canons of inquiry and knowledge and emphasize ideas and concepts mediated through words and symbols.[5]

After just one meeting, Terry could only hope that his school year would not be characterized by a hundred-days' struggle over what should be the curriculum for his new preschool classes.

DISCUSSION QUESTIONS

1. Should the United States adopt a mandatory, universal preschool program for all four-year-olds? If such a requirement is adopted, should it be done only in our public schools, or should we continue to rely heavily upon private programs that would be paid for by the government rather than tuition?

2. Should government-financed programs be provided only for poor children by expanding Head Start? This would leave the private sector to continue making available tuition programs for middle-class families.

3. If you were on the committee at East Banks Elementary School, what contributions would you make to the group's decision as to the appropriate curriculum for the new preschool program?

NOTES

1. P. Kutnick, "Does Preschool Curriculum Make a Difference in Primary School Performance? Insights into the Variety of Preschool Activities and Their Effects on School Achievement and Behavior in the Caribbean Island of Trinidad; Cross Sectional and Longitudinal Evidence," *Early Childhood Development and Care* 103, no. 1 (1994): 27–420 (accessed December 1, 2008, from Information World, www. informationworld.com/smpp/content~content=a746671312~DB=all).

2. L. Katz, "Curriculum Disputes in Early Childhood Education," *ERIC Digest*, University of Illinois, December 1999.

3. D. Crary, "Experts Bemoan Loss of Kids' Play Time," *Batavia Daily News*, November 25, 2008, A-6.

4. Crary, "Experts Bemoan Loss of Kids' Play Time."

5. D. J. Ferrero, "Pathways to Reform: Start with Values," *Educational Leadership* 62, no. 5 (February 2005): 10.

ADDITIONAL RESOURCES

Jacobson, L. "Children's Lack of Playtime Seen as Troubling Health, School Issue." *Education Week* 28, no. 14 (December 3, 2008). (ERIC Document Reproduction Service No. EJ820796.) Retrieved January 28, 2009, from ERIC database.

Swiniarski, L. "Starting School Early in Britain: A Model for Universal Preschool Education." *Early Childhood Education Journal* 35, no. 1 (August 2007): 19–24. Retrieved January 28, 2009, doi:10.1007/s10643-007-0182-7.

Zigler, E., and M. Finn-Stevenson. "From Research to Policy and Practice: The School of the 21st Century." *American Journal of Orthopsychiatry* 77, no. 2 (April 2007): 175–81. Retrieved January 28, 2009, doi:10.1037/0002-9432.77.2.175.

You Are Both the Judge and the Jury

How to Deal with Student Cheating

A 2008 Associated Press story cited the results of a new survey on student cheating and stealing. The Josephson Institute questioned almost thirty thousand students and reported the following results:

- 30 percent of U.S. high-school students have stolen from a store.
- 35 percent of boys and 26 percent of girls acknowledge stealing from a store in the past year.
- One in five said they stole something from a friend; 23 percent said they stole something from a parent or relative.
- 64 percent have cheated on a test.
- 64 percent cheated on a test in the last year.
- 38 percent cheated on a test two or more times in the last year— this is up from 60 percent and 35 percent in a 2006 survey.
- 36 percent said they used the Internet to plagiarize an assignment—this is up from 33 percent in 2004.[1]
- Perhaps even more alarming is the fact that "despite such responses, 93 percent of the students said they were satisfied with their personal ethics and character and 77 percent affirmed that 'when it comes to doing what is right, I am better than most people I know.'"[2]

Many schools have attempted to respond to these trends with programs often labeled as "character education." Although teachers have always attempted to teach and model moral and ethical behavior, character education actually introduces planned educational experiences to improve student behavior. At the same time, while teachers and administrators are trying to teach morals and ethics, they are also frequently cast in the role of being both a judge and a jury.

Monica Green was reviewing in her mind the series of events that had led to her current dilemma. One of her students, Joel Swick, had made arrangements to stay after school to take a make-up social studies exam, as he had been absent earlier in the week when the class had taken the test. On the morning he was scheduled to come in, Monica received an e-mail that there would be an emergency social studies department meeting after school. Such a meeting was unusual, and the department chair had not shared why the special meeting was necessary on such short notice. Having missed one department meeting earlier in the year, Monica felt compelled to attend the session that afternoon, especially since she could not help but wonder what the emergency could possibly be.

In thinking about her arrangement with Joel, she decided to ask her friend Linda Peabody, the school librarian, if she could help out. Monica knew that there was a workroom in the library that would be a quiet place for Joel to take his exam. She explained to her friend that she would not have to stay in the room the whole time as long as she checked in on the student occasionally.

With this arrangement made, Monica attended the meeting, where she learned one of her colleagues had announced that she was taking an early maternity leave. The prolonged discussion that followed dealt with whether the position should be offered to an experienced substitute who had served the district well or whether the vacancy should be publicized and opened to outside candidates. It was close to 4:30 p.m. when the group reached a consensus to recommend that the veteran substitute be hired. During the meeting Monica had forgotten about the time and her student in the library.

When she arrived back in her classroom, Linda was waiting for her, and was evidently upset. With Joel's exam in her hand, she told Monica she had left the room for approximately thirty minutes after he began taking the test. She had not intended to leave him so long, but she had gotten sidetracked helping another student with some research. When she went to check on the boy, he was writing an essay on a separate piece of paper with the test paper in front of him. Linda noticed that another paper was protruding from under the test.

Wondering if it was scrap paper, she walked over to Joel and gently pulled the paper out from under the test. It was obvious she had surprised him, because he stopped writing as she began examining the paper. Linda showed Monica what she had found. The page was filled on both sides with notes.

Although the handwriting was difficult to decipher, it was clear that the paper contained material related to American history, including names and dates. When Linda asked Joel what they were, he answered after a significant pause. When he finally responded, he said that they were the notes he had been studying before he came into the library, but he had forgotten about them when he entered the test room. He apologized and said that he knew he should have gotten rid of them before he started the test, but he assured Linda that he had not looked at them after he began the examination. It was obvious to Monica that her friend did not believe the boy and that she was anxious for Monica to compare the notes with what Joel had written on the test.

When she did so, it certainly seemed possible that her student had bene-fited from his notes. Along with possibly helping him to determine the answer on several multiple choice questions, he had written an essay that included specific facts from the notes. The question had asked the students to trace the events leading to the United States' entrance into World War I in 1917. In his essay, he had written sentences about the German use of submarine warfare. Using almost identical wording from his notes, the test essay referred to the sinking of the *Lusitania* in 1915 and how war had been averted until 1917. Both papers went on to note the sinking of the unarmed passenger ship, the *Sussex*, and quoted directly Woodrow Wilson's slogan in the presidential cam-paign of 1916 that the president "had kept us out of war."

Although the information was not on the sheet of notes, he included a paragraph in his essay that described the so-called Zimmerman Note to Mex-ico, which helped to fuel anti-German sentiment in the United States. Even if Joel had been cheating, he had obviously remembered this event without the help of his notes, but as she read the next paragraph there was another section where his essay was very similar to his notes. In this section he wrote about the fact that President Wilson sought a declaration of war because of the resump-tion of unrestricted submarine warfare in January of 1917.

As she thought about the possibility that there had been cheating, she considered the young man involved. Joel was a serious student whose parents pushed him hard to earn good grades. Monica's students knew that she liked to read specific facts in their essays. The chronology of events was, to her, important to assist students in understanding the causes and effects of historic events. Joel's essay on the United States' entrance into World War I was the most complete and well-documented one written by any student in the class. Other students had lost points for missing key events in their essays that dealt with the United States' entrance into World War I. This was not true of Joel, as he gained full credit for what he had written. Of course, if he had used his notes, it could have helped him not only on this essay, but also possibly on several of the objective questions.

As Monica thought about her student, she realized how very little she knew about him. He was very quiet in class and did not seem to socialize often with the other students. Thus far in the semester, he was carrying a 91 percent average, which would earn him an A- on his report card. Because of several questions the boy had asked Monica before the test, it was obvious that Joel was trying hard to earn an A. He had asked how she wanted the students to answer specific essay questions. There was no question that he was eager to write his essays in a way that would impress her. A colleague had told her that both of the boy's parents were teachers in another district and that they had been known to protest a grade given to their son if they felt it was unfair.

Before she could make a decision, Monica knew that she had to talk to her student. When she met with him the next day, Joel seemed extremely nervous, and before the conversation ended he seemed on the verge of tears. As he had done with Linda, Joel denied that he had used the sheet of notes while he had been taking the test. At the same time he admitted that he should have thrown the notes away before he began. Monica could not help but feel sorry for him and she ended the conversation. She told her student that she would continue to consider the situation and they would talk again tomorrow.

That evening she read the test again, and it was clear that given what he had written, the boy would receive a grade of 98 percent on the test, which was seven points higher than what he had received on any of his previous unit tests. The big question on Monica's mind was whether or not Joel was lying and if he had actually used the notes to answer any of the test questions. She was most concerned about the essay question dealing with World War I. It was evident that his answer included specific detailed information that was on the sheet of notes. It was these extra paragraphs that had helped him gain full credit for his answer on that question. She was convinced that his essay would have received a perfect score even from her college professor in American history. On the other hand, there were things in his answer that were not contained in his notes.

Monica knew that she would have to decide what to do that evening. If she determined that this was an incident of cheating, she would have to devise an appropriate punishment. If this happened, she would need to consider notifying Joel's parents, who very likely would support their son. Perhaps most disturbing was the fact that the incident seemed to be taking a toll on the boy. When she told her husband about her problem that evening, he observed that it looked like "you are both the judge and the jury."

DISCUSSION QUESTIONS

1. Is there anything else Monica might want to do before her next conversation with Joel?
2. Given the facts in the case, what would you do if you were the teacher?
3. Would you involve Joel's parents in this issue? Why? Why not? If you did contact them, what would you say?
4. Is there anything you can do when you begin working with a new class to reduce the possibility of cheating?

NOTES

1. D. Crary, "More High-School Students Admit They Lie, Cheat, and Steal," *Seattle Times*, 2008.

2. Crary, "More High-School Students Admit They Lie, Cheat, and Steal."

ADDITIONAL RESOURCES

Cromwell, Sharon. "What Can We Do to Curb Student Cheating?" *Education World* (2006).

Thompson, L. "Educators Blame Internet for Rise in Student Cheating." *Seattle Times* (2005).

A Difficult but Important Decision

A Recent Graduate Choosing Where to Apply for a Teaching Position

One of the first tough decisions faced by future teachers is which college to attend. Perhaps even more difficult is the one that occurs at the time of college graduation, and that is where to begin one's teaching career. Communities and school districts differ greatly, as do the salaries and benefits they offer. A teacher education graduate who is willing to look at the many professional opportunities available will find that choosing the right school is not easy. Along with selecting a job, new teachers must decide where to live. A significant percentage of teacher education graduates in the United States are Caucasian women who have attended suburban school districts. Many of the employment opportunities for new teachers are found in urban and rural communities. In addition, there are certain areas in the country where jobs are more plentiful if a graduate is willing to move to another state. There are also opportunities in private schools and, more recently, in charter schools.

Ashley Tanner had graduated with honors from a well-regarded suburban high school. Less than 5 percent of her senior class had been nonwhite students. A serious student, Ashley finished in the top 10 percent of her graduating class of 465 students. Since childhood, she had wanted to be an elementary teacher. As the oldest of three children, she often played school in her bedroom with her brother and sister, along with her mother, as her students. Her parents had bought her a small chalkboard, which she had used to teach her family.

When it was time for Ashley to choose a college, she decided on a small Christian institution on the other side of the city from where she lived. Despite the fact that her family did not live far from the campus, she and her parents decided that she should live in the college dormitory. While a freshman she had come home frequently, but as she gained friends and became active in college activities, Ashley began to spend most weekends on campus.

During her undergraduate years she had experienced a variety of school districts. One of her first classroom observation placements was in the city, where she worked with a superb master teacher. The school was located in a very poor neighborhood, but, at least in this particular first-grade class, the children seemed happy and well disciplined. It also appeared to Ashley that they were progressing well with their reading skills. Even though she had been only a sophomore at the time, she had been able to see herself as a teacher in this type of classroom. The fact that she would be working with children who were often living in poverty appealed to her missionary zeal, which had always been part of her motivation for becoming a teacher. It was difficult not to be sensitive to the needs of these children who most often came from low-income homes that made them eligible for free lunches and breakfasts at school.

Unfortunately, her second opportunity to work in such a classroom was not as positive. One of her two student teaching experiences had been in a sixth grade in another poor school in the city. Her master teacher was a veteran teacher, but it bothered Ashley that her primary classroom management method was to yell at the students. There were serious discipline problems in the class, and it was obvious that many of these students were resisting the teacher's management efforts. There was a degree of belligerence with some children and, to Ashley, their language was often shocking. Despite these drawbacks, she had developed a bond with many of the students, and her relationship with them was, in many ways, more positive than that of her master teacher. At the same time Ashley had to admit that she might have real difficulty dealing with a class such as this on her own. Even given this concern, she was still willing to consider working in an urban district.

When she moved to her second student teaching experience in a suburban district, it was easy for her to see the difference between this new assignment and her work in the city. This school was very much like the one she had attended, and she felt very at ease working with the children. The students were, for the most part, intelligent and highly motivated. There were only two who sometimes misbehaved, and neither of them would have been considered a serious disciplinary problem in her city classroom. A significant number of the students were reading above grade level, and both they and their parents were heavily invested in their schoolwork. The building itself was impressive, and the teachers she met all seemed to be conscientious and talented. Unlike in her urban setting, Ashley, as a student teacher, was given special attention, and the principal even offered to observe her teaching and ended up writing a recommendation for her. In their discussion following the lesson the principal recommended that, if possible, Ashley should continue after graduation and earn a master's degree in English language arts.

As she neared graduation, Ashley had decided to take the principal's advice and to continue her education at the same institution where she had earned her teaching degree. To save money she moved back to her parents' home and spent the next fifteen months working on her master's degree. With only four months left until her degree would be complete, she knew that it was time to begin considering where to send employment applications. During her final semester as a graduate student, she had already begun to think about her options. Her first thought was to consider her home school district and the suburban school where she had done her second student teaching assignment.

Using contacts she had in both of these districts, Ashley found that the job prospects in suburban districts were less than promising. It appeared that many veteran teachers were putting off retirement because of an ongoing recession and a serious downturn in the stock market. Because these districts paid the highest salaries of any school in the area, they were receiving hundreds of applications for the few positions available. With so many applicants to choose from, the successful candidates were likely to be teachers who had already proven themselves in another district.

Although she would certainly apply to work in these schools, to be realistic she knew that she needed to consider other alternatives. Because she had accumulated approximately $20,000 in debt during her five years of college, Ashley could not ignore the issues of salaries and fringe benefits. Next to the suburban schools, the best-paying district was the city. Although her home district started first-year teachers with a master's degree at $39,000, in the city the salary was $37,550. As she thought about applying to any city district, it was difficult to forget her very different experiences as a student. On the other hand, she did have several excellent references for her work in the city, and there seemed to be a greater need for teachers in most urban areas.

Recently, another possibility had come to her attention. During the past several years four charter schools had been established in the area. Ashley knew that the purpose of charter schools was to encourage educational innovation. Although they were publicly supported, these schools were free from most of the regulations that governed other public schools. In a panel discussion before her future teacher organization on campus, there had been both positive and negative comments about the local charter schools. Because these institutions received only a five-year charter, the schools were under pressure to meet specific educational objectives that were part of their charter application. In the seven years that these schools had been operating in her community, two of them had failed to have their charters renewed and their teachers had all lost their jobs. Although salaries were comparable to other urban schools in the area, some of the charters did not have the same fringe benefits. Two of them were run by for-profit companies that offered retirement options inferior to the other public schools. They also failed to offer the opportunity to earn tenure or to be represented by a teachers union.

In thinking about this option, Ashley remembered that the teachers from charter schools who had participated in the panel discussion were all extremely enthusiastic about their jobs. There was a new charter school opening in the coming fall a few miles from her home. Ashley was somewhat confident that with her master's degree, she had a chance of obtaining a teaching position at that school.

Another fallback possibility would be to apply for a job in a private school. As a Christian she knew she could feel comfortable in such a school. Ashley had been very impressed during an observation she did at St. Patrick's Catholic School during her junior year. The students were more diverse than the urban public school but they appeared to be well behaved. The children all wore uniforms and showed respect to their teachers and administrators.

The downside of taking a job in such a school was that, across the country, religious schools seemed to be closing in great numbers. In her own county the number of such schools had decreased while she was in college. At the same time, there was no question that teaching opportunities were available. The salary and fringe benefits offered by these schools were also much less lucrative than at any public school. Her investigation into this matter made it clear that she would be accepting a position that paid a maximum of two-thirds of the salary offered by a city school. Any public school would also offer superior medical coverage and retirement benefits. Her father had joked that if she ended up in one of these schools she would need to find a rich husband.

Another possibility would be to consider a rural school district. While attending college she had, on a number of occasions, spent weekends at the home of her roommate who lived on a farm. Her roommate, Brenda, had suggested that they both get a job in the district where she had gone to school. Located nearly twenty-five miles from the college and thirty-five miles from Ashley's home, her roommate's high school graduating class had only consisted of thirty-four students. Of this number Brenda had shared the fact that less than half of them had gone on to college. Most of these had gone to the local community college. While staying with her roommate, Ashley could not help but think how little seemed to be going on in the area where the school was located. The main street of the nearby village consisted of a gas station, a bar, a convenience store, a diner, and a newly opened small health club. Being a very large beet-producing area, the most important social event of the year in the town was the Beet Festival, which was highlighted by a parade and the annual crowning of the Beet Queen.

Ashley could not help but wonder whether or not she could be happy living in such a small town despite the fact that she had liked the people whom she had met. If she were able to share her housing cost with a roommate, it would be a way to save money, but Brenda had recently become engaged, and the possibility of having her for a roommate for an extended period of time seemed to have disappeared. Even if she found a small, single-bedroom apartment in the district, it would be much cheaper than living in the suburbs. She had made it a point to learn that the starting salary in the district was $32,000, which was better than any private school in the area.

The last possibility she felt a need to consider was leaving her home area and perhaps moving to another state where teaching jobs were more plentiful. A number of her friends from college had accepted teaching positions in North Carolina, Virginia, Nevada, and Texas. Others had left the country altogether. Her grandparents were living in Florida and had suggested that she come down there to live near them. Although she would find it hard to leave her family and friends, this was an option to consider if she had no appropriate offers from the schools in her community.

There were so many possibilities open to her, and she knew she had to narrow down her choices. There were references to collect, applications to fill out, and hopefully a number of interviews to schedule. All of this would undoubtedly add stress to her already busy life as a graduate student who was trying to complete her master's thesis. It was clear to Ashley that she would be facing a difficult but important decision over the next few months.

DISCUSSION QUESTIONS

1. What factors should a teacher candidate consider when attempting to choose a school district?
2. Given her situation, what strategy for finding a job do you think Ashley should employ?
3. What would be *your* top personal choices if you could pick any type of school and community to work in? Why?

ADDITIONAL RESOURCES

Klusmann, U., M. Kunter, U. Trautwein, O. Lüdtke, and J. Baumert. "Teachers' Occupational Well-Being and Quality of Instruction: The Important Role of Self-Regulatory Patterns." *Journal of Educational Psychology* 100, no. 3 (August 2008): 702–15. Retrieved March 24, 2009, doi:10.1037/0022-0663.100.3.702.

Seldin, A. "What Makes the Teaching of an African-American Urban Educator Exceptional?" *ERIC Database* (April 1999).

Skelton, C. "Failing to Get Men into Primary Teaching: A Feminist Critique." *Journal of Education Policy* 24, no. 1 (January 1, 2009): 39–54. (ERIC Document Reproduction Service No. EJ826691.) Retrieved March 24, 2009, from ERIC database.

Viadero, D. "Charters Seen as Lab for Report's Ideas on Teachers." *Education Week* (February 23, 2009).

Every Teacher Must Be a Teacher of Language Arts and Mathematics

Pressure on Teachers to Include Academic Subjects in Their Curriculum

The No Child Left Behind law mandates that public schools receiving Title I funds must test students annually in language arts and mathematics. This requirement covers most students in grades 3–8. The results of these examinations must be made public. There are consequences for schools that do not achieve what the law labels as adequate yearly progress. As a result, administrators throughout the nation have been seeking ways to place additional focus on these two subjects. In many schools, this has resulted in more classroom time spent on language arts and math. Another strategy has been to enlist teachers in every area of the curriculum to engage in interdisciplinary projects that will enhance the students' ability to be more successful on these tests. Such an emphasis provides a new challenge for music and art teachers.

As the chairperson of the fine arts program in the Castle Central School District, Lisa Moore realized that it was going to be her responsibility to bring together the music and art teachers in the district to discuss the recent message from their superintendent of schools. Following the release of some disappointing test scores in language arts and math, the superintendent had called a meeting of all of the district teachers and administrators. Prior to this session he made it clear that his remarks would be titled "Every Teacher Must Be a Teacher of Language Arts and Mathematics." During his speech he instructed every academic department to meet and devise a plan as to how they would better integrate language arts and math into their curriculum.

The meeting of the fine arts faculty brought together all twenty-five music and art teachers employed by the district. Among those representing music were faculty members assigned to teach elementary, middle school, and high school music courses, including those who were responsible for conducting the school band, orchestra, and vocal groups. To open the meeting, Lisa had repeated the superintendent's words concerning the need for all teachers to implement language arts and mathematics into their classes. Unfortunately, the meeting started out on a negative note when the first faculty member to speak appeared to be very upset about the reason for the meeting.

As the senior high band director, he announced to the group that "they hired me to conduct a band. They want me to have a marching band and perform at four football games and at three parades every year. In addition, I have to prepare for three public concerts with the concert band and also direct a jazz ensemble. Now they want me to teach reading, writing, and arithmetic?" The next person to raise a hand was a senior high art instructor who pointed out that he already had four different preparations each day, and reworking his lesson plans for all of these classes would be a very time-consuming.

Lisa was relieved when a middle school general music teacher shared the fact that she was already giving her students several writing exercises. She gave the example of her assignments to have students write biographical sketches of various composers. In addition, she had them write reflective essays concerning their reactions to various types of music. These assignments were given as a part of a unit on music appreciation.

The instructor for the music theory classes in the high school noted that there was a correlation between music and math and described how it entered into his teaching of intervals and chord progressions. As the discussion continued, it appeared that it was moving in a more positive direction when a senior high art teacher agreed that language arts and mathematics were an integral aspect of many of her art classes. Writing assignments dealing with specific art forms and artists could be added to her classes. She also noted that artists often use mathematics in planning their work.

At this point, a veteran middle school art teacher, who was vice president of the district's teachers union, gained the attention of the entire group with a rather controversial suggestion. He expressed his feelings that "if the district wants us to do serious curriculum work, they should pay us for it. Why don't we have a union representative request that the district have us all come in for a couple of weeks this summer and revise our curriculum? If they really are going to require us to do this right, we should be given time and compensation for doing the work."

The reaction to this recommendation was mixed. One young married teacher responded positively, saying, "Maybe then I could forget about a couple of weeks at my summer job." A faculty member who happened to have several children pointed out that one of the reasons she appreciated summer vacations was that it gave her time to spend with her family. She remembered that the last time the district had required a summer faculty workshop, it had been scheduled during the two weeks that her family had planned a time together at the lake. For her, at least, a summer workshop was not desirable.

Lisa thought it necessary to remind the department that they had been told to prepare a written report to the superintendent on how they were going to proceed in carrying out his instructions. In thinking about the summer workshop idea, it occurred to her that if the board of education agreed to pay the fine arts department for two weeks of summer work, they could expect to receive similar requests from other departments. This, plus the poor conditions of the local economy, seemed to make it very unlikely that the school district would grant such a request. To adjourn the meeting at this point with the idea that they petition the board would still leave the group with the responsibility of preparing a report.

In addition, she knew that even her own husband would question why teachers who worked only one hundred eighty days a year would require additional compensation for a one-hundred-ninety-day schedule. Of course, as a manager who often felt that unions were too greedy, he had little sympathy for many of the positions taken by her union. While she sometimes disagreed with him, she was aware that in the community, and, more important, in the board of education, there would be very little sympathy for teachers who were balking at a little extra work.

The discussion now moved in a different direction. A veteran secondary music teacher reminded the group that the high school had once offered a humanities class. It was a senior high elective that was team taught by a music, art, English, and history teacher. The curriculum was organized chronologically, and in every period of history each instructor taught how their discipline was affected by and affected the history of the period. The high school students who had taken the course had responded favorably to this interdisciplinary approach. The humanities experiment had ended when several of its teachers left the district. The fact that it required four faculty members made it an expensive elective, and this too had contributed to its demise.

However, the experience had demonstrated that interdisciplinary team teaching could be effective. It was also pointed out that this approach could be integrated at every level. Elementary classroom teachers could work with music and art teachers to plan projects that incorporated the arts into social studies as well as language arts. The teacher gave an example of a classroom teacher and an art teacher working together on a project that required the students to write a children's book that included illustrations done in art class. Another example was a social studies teacher and an art teacher working on an essay that was illustrated by a political cartoon. Lisa felt good that finally some specific lessons were being discussed and that many of the teachers present were participating by giving suggestions.

As it was nearing 5:00 a number of the teachers appeared to be getting restless, and it seemed that the group needed to formulate a plan to move forward. This occurred when the high school choral director pointed out that a good deal of professional literature was available that offered suggestions on how to meet the objective of integrating language arts and math into the fine arts curriculum. She thought it would be helpful if everyone did some reading on the issue. This could lead to some informal discussions about how the group could carry out the superintendent's mandate. A second suggestion came from a first-year teacher who said that there had been several excellent methods instructors at her college and, because they were close by, she was quite certain that they might have some ideas that would be helpful. She thought that they might even be willing to come to a meeting.

No one objected to coming back in two weeks after doing some homework. Many of them also thought it would be helpful to have some outside help. Lisa was happy that a next step had been agreed on, but she remained uneasy about how the whole issue would be resolved. She knew that it would be her responsibility to prepare the written response to the superintendent.

DISCUSSION QUESTIONS

1. Do you think it is appropriate and reasonable for music and art teachers to be asked to integrate language arts and math into their curriculum? Why or why not?

2. Choosing a specific grade level, outline a plan that allows students to experience either language arts or math in an art or music lesson.
3. Assuming that teachers of the fine arts should also be teachers of language arts and mathematics, how should districts seek to ensure that this objective is being met?

ADDITIONAL RESOURCES

Cornett, C. "Center Stage: Arts-Based Read-Alouds." *Reading Teacher* 60, no. 3 (November 1, 2006), 234–40. (ERIC Document Reproduction Service No. EJ749444.) Retrieved February 2, 2009, from ERIC database.

Raymond, A., and P. Broderick. "Teaching and Learning with the Arts." *Teaching Pre-K-8* 37, no. 6 (March 1, 2007): 36–39. (ERIC Document Reproduction Service No. EJ762720.) Retrieved February 2, 2009, from ERIC database.

Wiggins, D. "Pre-K Music and the Emergent Reader: Promoting Literacy in a Music-Enhanced Environment." *Early Childhood Education Journal* 35, no. 1 (August 2007): 55–64. Retrieved January 28, 2009, doi:10.1007/s10643-007-0167-6.

I Want to Design My Own Lessons

A District's Decision to Adopt a Scripted Language Arts Program

Choosing the most effective way to teach children to read has long been a controversial issue in the United States. The debate grew especially heated during the last quarter of the twentieth century, when those supporting the whole-language approach challenged the traditional methods that emphasize the use of phonics. By the end of the 1990s, many schools had settled on instructional plans that attempted to combine these two systems. With the signing of the No Child Left Behind Act in 2002, the question of the appropriate teaching techniques for teaching language arts again became an issue in schools throughout the nation.

One of the primary goals of the law has been to improve the reading skills of every student in the nation. To accomplish this, large amounts of money have been made available to states and individual school districts to promote the use of "scientifically validated" reading programs. In order to accomplish the lofty objective of making sure every child is proficient in reading by 2014, the legislation is relying heavily on a specific initiative titled Reading First. This section of the law makes funding available to schools that have adopted a language arts program that, in the view of the federal government, has been scientifically proven to be effective. One of the main criticisms of this initiative is that it has created scripted programs that limit the creativity of individual teachers.

Carol Lang was starting her second year as principal of the Whig Street Elementary School, and she had been instructed by her superintendent to establish a committee to study the various reading series that had been approved for funding under the Reading First program. The idea was that the group would choose the most appropriate program and prepare a Reading First grant proposal. Even though the superintendent was well aware that money for this program had been drastically reduced, it seemed wise to at least apply for a grant. If the district was unable to obtain federal money, he was prepared to fund locally any new language arts series that the committee recommended.

As a result of her formidable assignment, Carol had appointed a select committee made up of one veteran fifth-grade teacher, a second-year first-grade teacher, a special education teacher, and the district reading coordinator. In choosing the committee members, she had been careful to select people who were already knowledgeable in the field and who had demonstrated a sincere interest in language arts. Although she had only known them for a year, there was no question in her mind that they were respected members of the faculty. This was important, because Carol hoped that if the group could reach a consensus they would be able to more easily gain the support of the entire faculty. She had purposely kept the committee small in the hope that it would be easier to reach an agreement on a specific reading series.

Carol had given each of these individuals information on three of the most popular programs that had been approved by the federal education department. She had also requested that the committee members do some individual research concerning these programs. She had given them the month of September to do their homework.

Carol began the group's first meeting by restating the primary goal of the committee, but even before she introduced her first discussion question, she was interrupted by the fifth-grade teacher, Rob Miller. Rob was a well-known individual, not only within the school district but also in the community, who had been a member of the faculty for thirty-one years. In addition, he was a past president of the district's teachers union. In this capacity he had become known as a very effective and outspoken negotiator. When Rob entered the meeting, he had what appeared to be an armful of books and magazine articles. His first comment made it clear where he stood on adopting a new language arts series.

Rob began his remarks by saying, "I personally oppose what this committee is being asked to do. In reading through the materials you have given us, I find that each of these programs reduces the role of the teacher in that it gives us scripted lesson plans as well as assessments and increases the amount of irrelevant paperwork." This opening comment surprised the entire group. Rob then continued by tracing his own development as a teacher of reading. He noted how he had begun his career during the introduction of the whole-language system in schools across America.

Over the years he had taken what he felt was best of the whole-language ideas and combined them with a traditional, phonics-based approach. In doing so he reported that he had put together an outstanding classroom library and that his students were reading the best children's books available. They were also being taught to use context clues in identifying words that were new to them. In addition, he was assigning spelling words and writing assignments directly from the stories they were reading. At the same time, he was spending a significant amount of time teaching word recognition skills using phonics. As much as possible, he reported that he was individualizing his instruction to meet the needs of his students. Most of all, it was clear that the system he had developed was producing excellent test scores. Rob went on to say, "The bottom line is that I want to design my own lessons. Although it has taken many years, I have a system that I love and it works. To move to a prescribed program where I am reading lines out of a teacher's manual would be a step backward."

Without taking a breath, he referenced a book written immediately after the passage of No Child Left Behind. It was titled *Resisting Reading Mandates: How to Triumph with the Truth*, by Elaine M. Garan. He noted the author's concern about new pressures to force schools to use "commercial programs." He opened the book and read the following passage:

> Increasingly, people who have never even set foot in our classrooms and who do not know our students are telling us how to teach them. . . . You must follow the script because scientific research says you should. . . . The federal government has decided it knows better than we do, what we should teach, how we should teach, and even when we should teach it. . . . We are up against yet another one-size-fits-all, sure-fire, quick fix. . . . The latest buzzword is "science" . . . the carrot in the Bush plan is the promise of grants and other monetary benefits to those schools that get in line and use science. . . . If the science is infallible and yet some children still fail, then who is to blame? We, the teachers are.[1]

After he shared this portion of the book Rob went on to specifically criticize the Reading First program. He began by noting the dramatic reduction in funding for the program in the current federal budget. Even more important for him was the new evidence that the initiative was not working. To prove the point, he read to the committee from an article that appeared in the *Washington Post* in May 2008, which stated,

> Students enrolled in a $6 billion federal reading program that is the heart of the No Child Left Behind law are not reading any better than those who don't participate, according to a U.S. government report.
> The study released yesterday by the Department of Education research arm found that students in schools that use Reading First, which provides grants to improve elementary school reading, scored no better on comprehensive tests than their peers who attended schools that did not receive program money.
> The conclusion is likely to reignite the longstanding "reading wars."
> . . . House Appropriations Committee Chairman David R. Obey (D-WIS.) yesterday called Reading First a "failure." Sen. Edward M. Kennedy (D-MASS.), Chairman of the Senate education committee, said the administration "put cronyism first and the reading skills of our children last."[2]

From this article, Rob quickly moved to a story from the newspaper *USA Today* titled "Study: Bush's Reading First Program Ineffective."

> A $1 billion-a-year reading program that has been a pillar of the Bush administration's education plan doesn't have much impact on the reading skills of the young students it's supposed to help, a long-awaited federal study shows.
> The results, issued Thursday, could serve as a knock-out punch for the 6-year-old Reading First program.[3]

As soon as he finished reading from this article, Carol interjected that the district was well aware of the reduction in funding for Reading First, but that it was still by far the most important source of money available to help pay for a new language arts program. She also pointed out that it was going to be months, and maybe years, before the Congress and President Obama agreed on the conditions surrounding the reauthorization of No Child Left Behind, and whatever happened there was bound to be financial assistance for schools seeking to improve their language arts program.

Rob was quick to respond by claiming that the Department of Education had shown itself to be opposed to flexibility for teachers. He referred to a story that quoted Susan Newman, an assistant in the U.S. Department of Education, as saying that one of her objectives was to "end creative teaching." To be fair, he pointed out that the assistant secretary had claimed to have been misquoted and what she had really said was that she wanted to end "experimental teaching." But the reporter who wrote the story claimed that she really said that she wanted to end "creative teaching."[4]

Rob ended his remarks by saying, "I just believe that American education is headed down the wrong road. Teaching is more of an art than a science. Why can't we develop our own program that allows individual teachers the flexibility to use their own creativity?"

Colleen Anderson, the first-grade teacher, was the first to react to Rob's concerns. She was only in her second year of teaching, but she had already made a positive impression on her colleagues. In faculty meetings she had shown herself to be intelligent, articulate, and diplomatic. Carol could see in her the making of a future superintendent.

She began her remarks by praising Rob for his skills as a teacher and for the research he had done to prepare for the work of the committee. She then went on to say that as a new teacher she saw things somewhat differently. Her first year of teaching language arts had been a year of experimentation. The result was that she knew that mistakes had been made and that her students might have suffered. Like Rob, she had also brought in articles to share. Her first source was a study done by the American Federation of Teachers titled "Teaching Reading IS Rocket Science." The study was critical of teacher preparation programs in the field of language arts instruction. She shared the fact that her own preparation had been inadequate and that she entered her first classroom poorly prepared to teach reading.[5]

Rob did not disagree, but interjected that with adequate in-service instruction and help from experienced teachers, the district could develop its own framework for a program. The debate was on as Colleen shot back with, "You admitted that it took you a quarter of a century to develop a plan that worked for you. We don't have that much time. Every one of the series that we are looking at is the result of years of study by experts." She went on to extol what she felt were the virtues of a carefully prepared language arts series. For her, these programs provided a well-organized and complete approach to all phases of what we call language arts. They are sequenced by grade level and ready to use, even by a first-year teacher.

Rob rebutted this comment by suggesting that, because they were so tightly scripted, "You would not even need a teacher. We could put the teacher's script on a tape recorder." Colleen politely responded with, "When I have taught for thirty years, I might agree with you, but right now I could benefit from prepared lessons and assessments that have been tested and found to be successful."

At this point Barb Lewis entered the discussion. She had fourteen years of experience as a special education teacher. While admittedly there were many things about the proposed reading programs that she liked, she was not sure how they would work with her special education students. She went on to point out that everyone in her class had individualized education plans. Many of her primary students were not even ready for the first lessons in any of the series that were being suggested. In any case, her challenge would always be to individualize her instruction to meet the special needs of each student. It was hard for her to see how many of the standardized lessons and assessments would work with her special education students. She also asked that if anyone had noticed the frequency of the required assessments in all of the programs. It was clear that Barb was worried that, as a special education teacher, she already had more paperwork than she could handle and that the adoption of any of these new programs would only create more.

Up until now the meeting had been quite negative and Mary Johnson, the district's reading coordinator, decided that it should be her role to bring some balance to the discussion. As the person responsible for language arts instruction in the district, she had been facing significant pressures because of the stagnant reading scores of the students in the district during the past several years. She was well aware that the superintendent was expecting that the work of this committee would reverse that trend.

Mary's approach was to share an article published by the Harvard Graduate School of Education that quoted Diane Ravitch's summary of the work of the well-known reading expert Dr. Jeanne S. Chall. Dr. Chall had concluded that "no single method had completely solved the problems of teaching reading; some methods were better than others, but none was a panacea." With this in mind, Chall observed that although the debate was centuries old, it still needed to be continued.[6] Mary said, "We have begun such a debate today and although we do not presently agree on a way forward, we cannot quarrel with the need for our school district to constantly seek to improve what we are doing. With this goal in mind, I hazard to suggest that nothing would be lost by giving an audience to the representatives of the companies whose programs we have been asked to consider."

Carol quickly agreed with the reading coordinator, saying that "given the mandate of the committee, this needs to be done." She went on to say that she would arrange for a series of meetings to listen to presentations from each of the companies and that the sessions would be scheduled at a time when all of the members were free. With that, Carol quickly adjourned the meeting and watched as her four committee members silently left the conference room.

DISCUSSION QUESTIONS

1. What are your feelings about the position of the veteran teacher, Rob Miller, concerning "scripted language arts programs"?
2. How do you respond to the position taken by the new teacher, Colleen Anderson, in regard to such programs?
3. Do you feel that the concerns expressed by the special education teacher, Barb Lewis, are valid? Why or why not?
4. If you were a sixth member of this committee, what contributions might you make to the work of the group?

NOTES

1. E. M. Garan, *Resisting Reading Mandates: How to Triumph with the Truth* (Portsmouth, NH: Heinaenn, 2002) 1–2.

2. M. Glod, "Study Questions 'No Child' Act's Reading Plan," *Washington Post*, May 2, 2008, washingtonpost.com/wp-dyn/content/article/2008/05/01/AR200805010199. html (accessed January 7, 2009).

3. G. Toppo, "Study: Bush's Reading First Program Ineffective," *USA Today*, May 5, 2008, www.usatoday.com/news/education/2008-05-01-reading-first_n.htm (accessed January 7, 2009).

4. G. N. Schmidt, "Duncan Boosts Controversial 'Science' Claim about Early Reading Instruction," *The Resistance*, November 2002, www.substancenews.com/archive/Nov02/duncanboosts.com (accessed January 7, 2009).

5. "Teaching Reading IS Rocket Science," *AFT Teachers*, June 1999.

6. T. Mashberg, "More than One Way to Teach a Child to Read," *Ed.*, 2006, www. gse.harvard.edu/news_events/ed/2006/summer/features/chall.html (accessed January 7, 2009).

ADDITIONAL RESOURCES

Colt, S. "Do Scripted Lessons Work–Or Not?" *School by School Reform* (September 2005). www.pbs.org/makingschoolswork/sbs/sfa/lessons.html.

Gelberg, D. "Scripted Curriculum: Scourge or Salvation?" *Educational Leadership* 65, no. 6 (March 2008): 80–82. Retrieved February 23, 2009, from Academic Search Premier database.

McIntyre, E., E. Rightmyer, and J. Petrosko. "Scripted and Non-Scripted Reading Instructional Models: Effects on the Phonics and Reading Achievement of First-Grade Struggling Readers." *Reading & Writing Quarterly* 24, no. 4 (October 1, 2008): 377–407. (ERIC Document Reproduction Service No. EJ807330.) Retrieved February 27, 2009, from ERIC database.

Where Do I Start?

Establishing a Self-Contained Special Education Classroom

While there has been a clear trend in recent years to include special education students in general education classrooms, there remain many self-contained special education classrooms in our schools. Most often, these classes are made up of students who would have great difficulty succeeding in a more inclusive setting. Due to their disabilities, most of the children in these classrooms receive multiple special services. Among these services are speech, physical and occupational therapy, and counseling. At times, members of the class are pulled out frequently during the week to receive extra help. Added to this, some are mainstreamed with other children for classes such as art, music, or physical education. Others might be mainstreamed in the other academic subjects. Finally, under special education law, a self-contained classroom can include students who might otherwise be assigned to three different grade levels. As a result, a teacher might have five-, six-, and seven-year-olds in one class. All of these factors can create major organizational challenges to any teacher assigned to such a group.

Gretchen Elliot had graduated in May with a bachelor's degree and dual certification in elementary and special education. Although she had had several interviews during the spring and summer months and had been a finalist for two jobs, she was planning to begin the year as a substitute teacher. On September 1, Gretchen received a phone call from the principal of one of the schools where she had been a finalist. He told her that there was an immediate vacancy for a teacher in a primary, self-contained special education classroom. The teacher who was scheduled for that class had recently resigned in order to care for an ailing parent who lived in another state. Gretchen learned that the teacher had already left the area but had provided some preliminary notes for her replacement.

After a brief conversation with her new principal, Gretchen had been offered the position, which would begin the following Tuesday. This would give her five days to prepare to meet her new class. After her session with the principal she was given a tour of the school and taken down to her new classroom, where she was left to read the notes left by her predecessor.

In the notes she learned that the group was considered a self-contained eight-one-one class. Gretchen recalled that this meant that there was a limit of eight students, one teacher, and one aide. Thinking about her new challenge, it occurred to her that she had had little or no experience with such a class during her college preparation. The only memory she had was of observing a self-contained class of severely disabled students. About all she could remember from this brief visit was that she had felt so sorry for these children.

As she continued to read the notes, she learned that there was not only one teaching assistant, but an additional aide for one specific student. It was also mentioned that the occupational, speech, and physical therapists would be working with the children. Two of them would do "push-in" experiences regularly, and these times would have to be worked into the schedule. For all of her students there the goal was to have them with their "age-appropriate peers" as much as possible. In their individualized educational plans it was noted which of the children would be mainstreamed for special classes such as music and art. They also were to join their grade-appropriate peers for assemblies and field trips.

Because there were clear differences in the abilities of the students, it was impossible to plan frequent group lessons. Instead, with help from the aides, there would need to be time scheduled for small group and individual activities. Even before reading their individualized education plans, Gretchen knew that meeting the educational objectives of her six students would be an overwhelming challenge. Planning a typical day would in itself be difficult.

After considering the introductory notes, she was now ready to read the descriptions of the individual children. Since the teacher she was replacing had had most of the students the previous year, she had been able to leave a description of these students for Gretchen. A similar description was provided for the five-year-old by his preschool special education teacher.

- Matthew Stevens is eight years old and is considered to be a second grader. His special education classification is "speech impaired" and he receives speech and occupational therapy. Matt is a quiet boy who does not initiate conversation. He answers questions with one or two words and has serious receptive and language-processing problems. In addition, his fine motor skills are poor and his handwriting is difficult to read. He is reading at the kindergarten level but can only identify fifteen to twenty sight words. In math he can count as far as twenty-five. Personally, he is a polite and sensitive boy who is not often a discipline problem. On the other hand, he often comes to school tired and looking disheveled. His hair is often dirty, and he rarely wears clean clothes. Matthew contracted lice several times last year. Working with his parents has been difficult for previous teachers, as they have shown little interest in helping with homework or in communicating with the school. His attendance has been poor, as he seems to be the one responsible for getting himself on the bus in the morning. Matt is mainstreamed with Molly to a second-grade classroom for science and social studies. A teacher's assistant accompanies both students to these classes.
- Annie Johnson is six years old and considered a first grader. Her classification is "speech impaired" and she receives services in speech and counseling. Annie is currently living in a foster home, as she was removed from her home at the end of April. Before being taken into foster care she attended two other schools prior to her parents' moving into this district. Like Matt, she has serious language problems and is also reading at the kindergarten level. In a test at the end of last year she was able to identify fifteen letter sounds and nine sight words. She can count to twenty with some prompts. Her behavior can be defiant, and she has difficulty following school rules. In addition, there are often conflicts with her peers, and she can be aggressive with adults as well as children. Her best performance occurs when she is working one-on-one with an adult, but even then she can become moody and uncooperative. When Annie has visits with her parents, it sometimes negatively affects her behavior for several days. All of last year she met with a school counselor, who was attempting to help her identify her feelings and improve her relationship with her peers.

• Molly Ashdown is seven years old and considered to be in second grade. Her special education classification is "learning disabled," and she receives special services in speech, occupational therapy, and physical therapy. She is reading at the kindergarten level and has great difficulty in all academic areas. Her problems include a poor memory as well as serious difficulty with processing new material. In addition to her language problems she appears to be delayed in fine motor and gross motor skills. There is a possibility that Molly's mother might have used drugs and/or alcohol during her pregnancy. She is easily distracted and has been prescribed medication for attention deficit disorder. She does not always receive her medication regularly at home. Personally, she is a cooperative child who is outgoing with other people. She talks easily with adults and likes to mother younger children in the classroom. Molly is a very likable girl but still is not readily accepted by her peers. She does not seem to have the age-appropriate social skills and is occasionally picked on by other students outside of the classroom.

• Colin Leathersich is seven years old and considered to be in first grade. His special education classification is "other health impairment," and his special services include speech, occupational therapy, and counseling. Although Colin has been diagnosed as suffering from attention deficit disorder, his parents have refused medication, as they claim they do not see his behavior to be a problem. In the classroom he is always moving and is extremely impulsive. Colin needs to be watched very carefully on the playground because he is very capable of doing things that might cause an injury to himself and to others. He works best with one-on-one instruction and needs constant repetition. In addition, he is easily distracted and has difficulty waiting for his turn when in a group. As a result, Colin can frequently be disruptive.

• Paul DeAngelo is seven years old and considered to be a first grader. He is classified as being "autistic" and receives services in speech, occupational therapy, physical therapy, and music therapy. Academically, Paul does very well. He is at or above grade level in all areas but has problems with reading comprehension. His expressive language is very limited. Due to his autism he has always had a very structured program with a picture schedule that goes everywhere with him. He has shown great progress with behavior issues but has great difficulty with change and will shut down when a new situation arises for which he has not been prepared. Paul sometimes has outbursts, and it can take up to thirty minutes to calm him down when he becomes upset. His schedule must be consistent every day, and he performs best when things are well structured in the classroom. Social stories are used daily to prepare him for upcoming situations. His teachers have all agreed that Paul is usually friendly but most often plays alone. He has an obsession with trains and talks about them constantly. He is also extremely interested in music and has responded well to music therapy. As a result of his autism, Paul has a one-on-one teaching assistant who helps him with his picture schedule, daily routine, and behavior plan. It will be a very time-consuming task for any teacher to plan Paul's day. This is especially true if there are alterations in the daily schedule for the class.

• Max Leonardo is five years old and considered to be a kindergarten student. His special education classification is "other health impairment." Each week he is scheduled for speech, occupational therapy, and physical therapy. Max has serious articulation problems, and he is very difficult to understand when he speaks. When he senses that people cannot understand him, he becomes frustrated and angry. He has poor muscle control and balance, along with difficulties with almost any bodily movement. His individual-ized education plan calls for five and a half hours of therapy per week, some of which is done in the classroom, while on other days he is pulled out for individual sessions. Max currently does not know his shapes or colors. He is working on learning to write his name but cannot yet identify all of the letters in his name. He can count to five but cannot identify the number five with consistency. Socially, he is friendly and very animated. He is known by many in the school and appears to be very popular with a significant number of adults.

After reading the descriptions of her new students, Gretchen felt like she was about to cry. Her mixed emotions ranged from concern for the children to panic over how she would work with such a group. It occurred to her that somehow she was going to have to try to meet with her aides, and hopefully the specialists dealing with her children, as soon as possible. In addition, she knew that she had to read each of their individual education plans before she met with the class. It occurred to her that there might be someone else in the school with whom she could talk about her students before she met with them next week. Despite the magnitude of the challenge, Gretchen was determined to do whatever was necessary to succeed in this, her first teaching assignment. She had been working toward this moment for many years, and it was important that she make the most of it. Although she had not mentioned it to her principal, Gretchen felt quite unprepared to be in charge of her new classroom. In fact, she could only ask herself, "Where do I start?"

DISCUSSION QUESTIONS

1. What can Gretchen do that would help her to prepare for meeting her class the following week?
2. When she does meet them, what issues will she need to deal with on the first day?
3. Do you support the continuation of providing self-contained special education classrooms such as the one described in this case study? Why or why not?

ADDITIONAL RESOURCES

Merritt, R. "Self-Contained Classrooms" (pp. 1-1). Great Neck Publishing (2008). Retrieved March 9, 2009, from Research Starters–Education database.

Ousley, O. "Are General Education Classrooms or Special Education Classrooms Better for a Child with Autism?" ABCNEWS.com (October 23, 2008). abcnews. go.com/Health/AutismLiving/story?id=5975241.

"The Right Stuff." *Technology & Learning* (October 2008). Retrieved March 24, 2009, from Academic Search Premier database.

I Don't Want to Start a Big Controversy

A Faculty Discussion Concerning Controversial Issues

Decisions teachers make in their classrooms can embroil them in controversial issues within their school and community. This is true at every grade level and in almost all subject areas. As a result, faculty members must be sensitive to the fact that their freedom to do and say what they want in their own classroom is limited. These limitations can be the result of laws, district policies, and court decisions. At other times they result from the culture of the school and community, which could affect a teacher's academic freedom. Because of these factors, it is extremely helpful for teachers to be familiar with the law as well as with the values in their community. Finally, they should know that before making a decision on a controversial issue, it is wise to talk with those who are responsible for the school program.

The discussion occurred at what had been labeled "the Rookie Table" in the faculty dining room. It just so happened that four of the first-year teachers at Southern Lake High School had the same lunch period. The group members were from different departments, but they had made it a practice to eat together most days. For them, it had become a good time to unwind and to share their daily problems. A veteran teacher, who often ate at an adjoining table, had labeled them "the Rookie Table," and the group had even made their own sign, which was placed on the table each day.

The conversation yesterday had been especially lively. Austin Matthews, a social studies teacher, had begun the exchange by telling about a discussion that had occurred in his advanced placement American history class. He had been trying to encourage his students to become concerned about current events and had adopted the practice of taking five minutes at the beginning of each class to talk about the major news stories of the day. Yesterday he had begun the discussion by noting that following the 2008 election, the Democratic Party had gained control of both houses in the state legislature. He asked the class to consider what impact this might have in their state.

The first student responded that "the Democrats are pretty much all socialists, and it probably means that the state will pass more laws and regulations limiting free enterprise." He went on to say that "they might even try taking over some of the businesses in the state." A young lady in the class, who had indicated in an earlier discussion that she was a Democrat, took issue with her party being called socialists. She responded with, "If the Democrats are socialists, then the Republicans are laissez-faire conservatives. In case you haven't noticed, this philosophy has ruined our economy over the last eight years."

A third student, Brad Lewis, a young man who was very interested in politics, entered the discussion by suggesting that both of his classmates were wrong. He noted that because of the current recession both parties have become Keynesian economists. It was clear that this statement confused most of the students, so Austin had asked Brad to explain what he meant. As part of his explanation, he pointed out that both parties had recently supported stimulating the national economy by bailing out a large number of the nation's failing banks. At the same time, it now appeared that Congress was establishing more stringent regulations on banks and other financial institutions. He went on to share with the class the fact that both parties in their state had requested federal financial assistance, even if it meant added regulations. Austin told his friends that he had been enjoying the exchange until a fourth student had quieted everyone by asking the question, "Mr. Matthews, where do you stand politically? Are you a Democrat or a Republican?"

Austin told his friends at the lunch table, "For what seemed like an eternity I was speechless." One of his friends at the table interrupted his story by observing that "I am surprised they don't already know that you are a flaming liberal Democrat." Austin responded by saying he had been trying to be careful about sharing his personal political opinions with his class. Another one of his colleagues asked him, "How did you respond to the kid's question?" Austin answered by saying he told the students, "I'm not sure that it is appropriate for me to share my political preferences. And then I closed the discussion and began talking about the American Revolution. Even though that ended the conversation today, I expect they will keep asking."

Amber Estanatos, the choral music teacher at the school, entered the discussion suggesting that history is not the only subject where controversy can arise. She shared the fact that when she was preparing for her winter concert, it had been her hope to have the chorus sing a piece by John Rutter. Amber pointed out that Rutter is a British composer who writes music that is often sung in Anglican churches around the world. "The lyrics in the piece I wanted to use had a Christian connotation, even though it was not a Christmas carol as such." She shared the fact that one of the colleagues in her department claimed that the piece could still upset some community members and maybe even one or more students. Amber said that rather than creating a problem, they had sung "Silver Bells" instead.

Neil Heath, an English teacher, said, "I was troubled at Christmas as well." He noted that "I have a small artificial Christmas tree at home that I would have liked to put in my classroom, but because I didn't see any Christmas decorations in the school, I decided to forget it. As an English teacher, I also have a problem with what books I can assign or put on my reading list. I have in my briefcase a list of the books that have created controversy in various schools. I've got it right here; let me show it to you." The group was somewhat incredulous when they saw the following list:

- Mary Rodgers's *Freaky Friday*: "Makes fun of parents and parental responsibility."
- George Eliot's *Silas Marner*: "You can't prove what that dirty old man is doing with that child between the chapters."
- William Shakespeare's *Macbeth*: "Too violent for children."
- Herman Melville's *Moby Dick*: "Contains homosexuality."
- Anne Frank's *Diary of a Young Girl*: "Obscene and blasphemous."
- E. B. White's *Charlotte's Web*: "Morbid picture of death."
- Robert Louis Stevenson's *Treasure Island*: "You know what men are like and what they do when they've been away from women that long."
- J. R. R. Tolkien's *The Hobbit*: "Subversive elements."
- Roald Dahl's *Charlie and the Chocolate Factory*: "Racist."
- *Webster's Dictionary*: "Contains sexually explicit definitions."[1]

He then shared a second list of additional books that also noted why they had been censored.

- *It's Perfectly Normal* by Robie H. Harris for homosexuality, nudity, sex education, religious viewpoint, abortion, and being unsuited to age group.
- *Forever* by Judy Blume for sexual content and offensive language.
- *The Catcher in the Rye* by J. D. Salinger for sexual content, offensive language, and being unsuited to age group.
- *The Chocolate War* by Robert Cormier for sexual content and offensive language.
- *Whale Talk* by Marilyn Reynolds for sexual content.
- *What My Mother Doesn't Know* by Sonya Sones for sexual content and being unsuited to age group.
- *It's So Amazing! A Book about Eggs, Sperm, Birth, Babies, and Families* by Robie H. Harris for sex education and sexual content.[2]

Neil told the group that there were at least three books on these lists that he would like to assign to his students, or at least put on a reading list.

Richard Collazzi, the science teacher in the group, was the last to share his concerns. He claimed that he had to deal with the most controversial issue of all. He noted that "in just about a month I will be introducing Darwin's theory of evolution. I am very worried about students asking me about intelligent design and/or biblical creationism." He went on to say that "neither of these topics is mentioned in the state curriculum or in my textbook." He shared his worry that his students would ask about these alternative theories and perhaps even inquire about his personal beliefs. Because of the church and state issue, he felt that he was in an even more dangerous position than being asked if he was a Democrat or a Republican.

It was at this point that the bell rang and they all left for their next class. The questions that had come up during their lunchroom conversation were left unanswered, but they all knew that at some point they would have to find the answers.

DISCUSSION QUESTIONS

1. How do you think Austin, the social studies teacher, should deal with the question concerning his political party affiliation?

2. What should teachers do to find answers about religious issues that emerge in their work? If asked, should they share their religious beliefs with students?

3. Teachers need to be sensitive concerning assigned readings and recommended Internet sites. What is the best way to avoid becoming involved in a controversy related to the learning materials used in classes?

4. In what ways can a teacher gain assistance in finding answers to the types of questions raised in this case study?

NOTES

1. D. M. Sadker, M. P. Sadker, and K. R. Zittleman, *Teachers, Schools, and Society* (Boston: McGraw-Hill, 2008), 245.

2. *The Most Frequently Challenged Books of 2005*, Office for Intellectual Freedom, American Library Association, www.ala.org/ala/oif/bannedbooksweek/challengedbanned/challengedbanned/htm.

ADDITIONAL RESOURCES

Coury, J. G. "Controversial Issues in the Classroom." Karen's Linguistics Issues (2001). www3.telus.net/linguisticsissues/controversial.html.

Crouch, R., and D. Abbot. "Is Green Education Blue or Red? State-Level Environmental Education Program Development through the Lens of Red- and Blue-State Politics." *Journal of Environmental Education* 40, no. 3 (Spring 2009): 52–62. Retrieved March 24, 2009, from Academic Search Premier database.

Dillon, S., R. Cathcart, B. Driehaus, S. Hamill, G. Kovach, and K. Zezima. "Classrooms Find Lessons in Obama's Inauguration." *New York Times* (January 16, 2009). Retrieved March 24, 2009, from Academic Search Premier database.

They Want Me to Be the Advisor

A Teacher Being Asked to Advise a Gay-Straight Alliance Club

Most high schools have a number of student clubs and organizations as part of their extracurricular programming. Some of these groups are found in almost every school. These would include a student council, a yearbook staff, an honors society, a drama club, and perhaps even a school newspaper. Other groups might arise and disappear, depending on the level of student interest. A school organization can be formed because of the initiative of a faculty member or sometimes as the result of the interest shown by one or more students. A teacher interested in chess or debate might find a group of students who had a similar interest. Advisors of some of the larger established clubs are often paid extra compensation, while teachers working with less formal groups are not given extra salary. It is not unusual for a faculty member to be asked to advise a group that is attempting to organize.

After going to a movie, Nathan Jacobia and his girlfriend, Cherish Zaccari, stopped for a snack at a local coffee shop. When they had been served, Nathan said, "You won't believe what happened to me today." Cherish responded by saying, "You seem to have a new story every day." It was easy for her to see by his expression that this was a special story, especially after he had told her that he had been approached by three students to become the advisor for a new club. Her initial reaction was that it was quite flattering for a second-year social studies teacher to be asked to work with a student group. She commented, "It must mean that they like you. What is the new club they want you to advise?"

When he answered her question, it was evident that he was concerned. The students who had visited him wanted to begin a chapter of the Gay-Straight Alliance. She had never heard of the group, but was able to guess what it was. Nathan told her that he had not given the students a definitive answer and that after school he had gone on the computer to find out as much as he could about the organization. He took out of his pocket a folded sheet of paper for her to read. On the first sheet was an article that began by addressing the question "What Is a Gay-Straight Alliance?" Together they silently read the following:

A Gay-Straight Alliance (GSA) is a student-run club, typically in a high school, which provides a safe place for students to meet, support each other, talk about issues related to sexual orientation, and work to end homophobia. Many GSAs function as a support group and provide safety and confidentiality to students who are struggling with their identity as gay, lesbian, bisexual, transgender, or questioning. In addition to support, some GSAs work on educating themselves and the broader school community about sexual orientation and gender iden-tity issues. They may bring in outside speakers to cover a particular topic such as GLBTQ [Gay, Lesbian, Bisexual, Transgender, and Questioning] history. They may organize a "Pride Week" or "GLBTQ Awareness Events" and offer a series of educational workshops, panels, and pride celebrations. Many participate in the Day of Silence, a day when participants remain silent all day as a way of acknowledging the silence induced by homophobia in our society. Some GSAs organize a "Teach the Teachers" staff development day which focuses on teach-ing school staff how to be better allies for GLBTQ students. For example, GSA members would present scenarios about discrimination or harassment and get teachers to brainstorm about how to respond to those situations.

Other GSAs are activist clubs and have worked to get GLBTQ issues repre-sented in the curriculum, GLBTQ-related books in the library, and progressive non-discrimination policies implemented at a district level. All of these differ-ent types of GSAs also provide a social outlet for GLBTQ students and their straight allies. Lots of GSAs organize barbeques or movie nights, go to the Gay Prom in Hayward or the GLBTQ Pride Parade in San Francisco, and attend con-ferences together. GSAs are a great way to build community at your school and lessen the isolation that GLBTQ students might otherwise experience.[1]

After reading this material, Cherish asked, "Do you think that nonhomo-sexual students would join such a club at East Side High School?" They both knew that the school was located in a heavily conservative Republican suburb. It was primarily a blue-collar community that contained many older citizens and a number of evangelical churches. Cherish couldn't help but wonder how the majority of the residents would react to having such a club in their school. Nathan was also concerned about how the students would respond. He did tell her that one of his three visitors had made it clear that she was not a homosexual and that she had some other friends who were straight and who would be interested in joining the club.

Cherish raised another question concerning whether the school's principal would allow the formation of a Gay-Straight Alliance in his school. Nathan replied with, "I am not sure that he has the power to stop such a group from meeting in the school." In support of this position he told her about his conversation after school with Brianne Alderman, an English teacher down the hall. She told the story of how two years ago she had been asked to work with a group that wanted to start an after-school Bible study. Brianne shared the fact that she thought the administration was reluctant to approve of such a group. After consulting with the school attorney they had learned that the district could not prohibit students from having a Bible study club if other groups were allowed to use the building for after-school meetings. The only restriction, according to the lawyer, was that the faculty member attending the meetings could not lead or actively participate in the discussion.

Nathan went on to explain that the American Civil Liberties Union was involved in defending the right of students to form a Gay-Straight Alliance chapter in their schools. They were using as the basis of their defense the federal Equal Access law, and they were winning their cases. It is the argument of the American Civil Liberties Union that "Gay-Straight Alliances foster tolerance and help students who have traditionally been marginalized feel safe and valued. Schools not only shouldn't discriminate against GSAs, they should be encouraging them to form."[2]

As they continued their discussion on how a Gay-Straight Alliance club would be organized, Nathan showed Cherish a plan that he had found on the Internet. Together they read through the steps that were recommended in forming such a club.

---

1. Follow Guidelines: Establish a GSA the same way you would establish any other group or club. Look in your Student Handbook for the rules at

your school. This may include getting permission from an administrator, finding an advisor, and/or writing a constitution.

2. Find a Faculty Advisor: Find a teacher or staff member whom you think would be supportive or who has already shown themselves to be an ally around sexual orientation issues. It could be a teacher, counselor, nurse, or librarian.

3. Inform Administration of Your Plans: Tell administrators what you are doing right away. It can be very helpful to have an administrator on your side. They can work as liaisons on your behalf with other teachers, parent groups, community members, and the school board. If an administrator is resistant to the GSA, let them know that forming a GSA club is protected under the federal Equal Access Act.

4. Inform Guidance Counselors and Social Workers about the Group: These individuals may know students who would be interested in attending the group.

5. Pick a Meeting Place: You may want to find a meeting place which is off the beaten track at school and offers some level of privacy or confidentiality.

6. Advertise: Figure out the best way to advertise at your school. It may be a combination of school bulletin announcements, flyers, and word-of-mouth. If your flyers are defaced or torn down, do not be discouraged. Keep putting them back up. Eventually, whoever is tearing them down will give up.

   Besides, advertising for your group and having words up such as "gay, lesbian, bisexual, transgender, or questioning" or "end homophobia" or "discuss sexual orientation" can be part of educating the school and can actually make other students feel safer—even if they never attend a single meeting.

7. Get Food: This one is kind of obvious. People always come to meetings when you provide food!

8. Hold Your Meeting! You may want to start out with a discussion about why people feel having this group is important. You can also brainstorm about things your club would like to do this year.

9. Establish Ground Rules: Many groups have ground rules in order to insure that group discussions are safe, confidential, and respectful. Many groups have a ground rule that no assumptions or labels are used about a group member's sexual orientation. This can help make straight allies feel comfortable about attending the club.

10. Plan for the Future: Develop an action plan. Brainstorm regarding activities. Set goals for what you want to work toward. Contact Gay-Straight Alliance Network in order to get connected to all of the other GSAs, get supported, and learn about what else is going on in the community.[3]

After they had read through the entire list, Cherish asked Nathan what he was going to do about the students' request. He replied, "I'm not sure, but I know they will be back for an answer tomorrow afternoon."

DISCUSSION QUESTIONS

1. Do you think that it is appropriate for the government to force local school districts to allow Gay-Straight Alliance organizations or clubs to meet in schools?
2. Should school administrators have the power to regulate the activities of a Gay-Straight Alliance club in their building? If so, what kind of restrictions should they be allowed to place on such an organization?
3. If you were Nathan, what would you do about the students' request?

NOTES

1. "How to Start a Gay-Straight Alliance," GSA Network, www.gsanetwork.org/resources/start.html (accessed February 9, 2009).

2. "ACLU Applauds Georgia Students' Gay-Straight Alliance Victory," American Civil Liberties Union, March 22, 2005, www.aclu.org/lgbt/youth/12180prs20050322.html (accessed February 9, 2009).

3. "How to Start a Gay-Straight Alliance."

ADDITIONAL RESOURCES

Garden, N. *Hear Us Out: Lesbian and Gay Stories of Struggle, Progress and Hope, 1950–Present.* New York: Farrar, Straus, and Giroux, 2007.

Safe Schools Program for Gay and Lesbian Students. *Massachusetts Department on Elementary and Secondary Education* (November 20, 2007). www.doe.mass.edu/cnp/safe/ssch.html.

Word, R. "Students Challenge School's Gay Club Ruling in Florida." *USA Today* (March 6, 2009). www.usatoday.com/news/education/2009-03-06-gay-alliance_N.htm.

Teachers Versus Machines

Should We Be Spending Money on Technology or Additional Teachers?

Whenever there are significant economic problems, nationally or in individual school districts, there most often is a need to reduce school budgets. This has certainly been true with the recession that began in 2008. Schools throughout the nation have faced reductions in their state aid and have experienced difficulties in raising enough money from local property taxes. Since a high percentage of the revenues for most districts comes from property taxes, the current housing and mortgage crisis has caused severe problems for many school districts. The result has been heated debates over the best way to reduce spending. Because much of the curriculum and other costs are mandated or merely necessary for operation, the expenditures available for reduction are limited. With the majority of school budgets dominated by salaries and fringe benefits, these categories must be considered. The fact that specific personnel issues and benefits are usually regulated by negotiated contracts with employee unions also limits the options available to boards of education. In any organization, the elimination of jobs will be an emotional issue that will involve employee unions.

Chris Bond is a fifth-year physics teacher at North Ridge High School. He loves his job and spends much of his free time planning lessons and labs, grading papers, and advising a science club that he has formed. During his relatively brief tenure at North Ridge, Chris has developed a reputation as a champion of technology. As a second-year teacher he became the first faculty member in the school to use a SMART Board as an integral part of his teaching. Chris has filled his classroom and laboratory with a variety of technology, some of which he has purchased with his own money.

A year ago his reputation as a supporter of the use of educational technology had been further enhanced when he became involved in a district-wide debate over the use of cell phones in school. North Ridge had been considering a ban on all student cell phones in the building. At a public board of education meeting, a significant number of parents had argued that a cell phone helped them to communicate with their children concerning urgent family business. Other parents had expressed concern over the security of their children and believed that the cell phone might be helpful even if it was banned for use in the classroom.

At the meeting Chris had spoken in favor of cell phones, pointing out that they could be used as an instructional tool. He quoted a research study suggesting "that mobile phones could in fact come to be perceived as natural in the school setting as any other technology." Having been asked by a member of the audience to give an example of how a cell phone could be used for instructional purposes, Chris read the following list to those attending the meeting:

- timing experiments with stopwatch
- photographing apparatus and results of experiments for reports
- photographing development of design models for e-portfolios
- photographing texts/whiteboards for future review
- bluetoothing project material between group members
- receiving SMS and e-mail reminders from teachers
- aynchronizing calendar/timetable and setting reminders
- connecting remotely to school learning platform
- recording a teacher reading a poem for revision
- accessing revision sites on the Internet
- creating short narrative movies
- downloading and listening to foreign language podcasts
- logging into the school e-mail system
- using GPS to identify locations
- transferring files between home and school[1]

He ended his argument by referring to a New York Times article that pointed out that cell phones are "a device kids have, it's a device they are familiar with and want to take advantage of." This same article pointed out that "the only difference now between smartphones and laptops . . . is that cell phones are smaller, cheaper, and more coveted by students."[2]

While many of his fellow teachers disagreed with him about trying to use cell phones in the classroom, his reputation as a supporter of technology had only grown as a result of his comments at the meeting. It now appeared that he might be called on again to champion the use of educational technology in his school. Chris had just heard about a teacher union meeting scheduled for the next day. The purpose of the session was to develop a union position on what type of budget cuts should be considered for the coming year.

For weeks there had been rumors about the possible elimination of both teaching and nonteaching positions in the district. It was thought that because of reduced enrollment in the high school, these cuts would come primarily from the high school faculty. Although no decisions had been made, the executive council of the union decided to solicit opinions of the membership.

At lunch that day Chris had talked to Jane Voorhees, a member of the English faculty, who had let him know that she would be suggesting cuts in his favorite area of the budget. Her examination of this year's budget had revealed that the school district was spending over $500,000 annually on technology. Jane pointed out that the largest single part of the technology budget was for the instructional technology staff. This included at least one instructional technology specialist in every building as well as several managers in the central office. Some of these individuals acted as aides in the computer labs, while others provided technical or curricular support. Even though Chris knew some of these people, he had never been aware of the size of the instructional technology staff.

Along with the personnel cost, significant amounts were budgeted for new and replacement equipment as well as for educational software. The district was in the second year of a five-year plan to put a SMART Board in every classroom. There was also an ongoing initiative to triple the number of wireless computers available in the district.

Chris knew that Jane was not a fan of technology and that a computer in her classroom was seldom used. For her, English education was about learning to write effectively and to read fine literature. She let him know that it was her intention to recommend at the meeting that the union urge the board of education to reduce spending on technology rather than to release faculty members. To her, the choice was simple. Keeping class sizes smaller was a better way to help students learn than buying more computers or SMART Boards. In her mind, and undoubtedly in the minds of other faculty members, it was a question of teachers versus machines.

Jane told Chris that she was planning to share information that supported the idea of smaller classes as a way to improve academic achievement. It was her intention to distribute at the meeting a summary of the Star Study that had taken place in Tennessee. Her handout, which she shared with Chris, included the following information:

> STUDY DESIGN: This long-term, statewide study included 79 schools, 328 classrooms, and about 6,300 students. Student achievement was compared in three types of classrooms: standard classes (a certified teacher and more than 20 students; supplemented classes (one teacher and a full-time, non-certified teacher's aide); and small classes (one teacher and about 15 students). Since that time this study has continued to develop and is now seen as the "largest, best-designed field experiment that has ever appeared for education." Initially, student achievement was assessed in each of their first years in school. The students were then followed into the higher grades and their academic records were monitored.
>
> STUDY FINDINGS: Results from standard classes and supplemented classes were quite similar. This means that there were few advantages in terms of student achievement from simply having untrained aides in classrooms. Results in the small classes were noteworthy. There were substantially higher levels of student achievement. The gains were also higher for those students who were in small classes for more years. In addition, the small class advantages were found for all types of students, and they were quite similar for boys and girls. Students from poverty, African-American students, and inner-city students had even greater gains. The findings from the follow-up studies as the small-class students moved into secondary schools are more significant. The small-class students earned better grades, fewer dropped out of school, fewer were retained, and once they were in high school, more took foreign languages and advanced-level courses, more were found to be in the top 25 percent of their classes, and more graduated from high school.[3]

Chris read through her handout and found it quite convincing. But later that day, when researching the study, he learned that the smaller class sizes in the study were only in grades K–3. Other studies on the impact of smaller class sizes at the high school level were less convincing. On the other hand, he knew that both teachers and parents would support the idea of smaller classes and expected that most students would agree.

He could not help but conclude that his colleague would make a very convincing argument that it might be best to cut the district's technology budget as opposed to reducing faculty. She was prepared to suggest that any cuts in technology would not have to be permanent, but during the current budget crisis this area of the budget should be looked at very carefully. Chris thought it had been very thoughtful for Jane to tell him of her intentions before the meeting. In doing so she was giving him the chance to develop counterarguments. As he considered what could become a debate on the subject, it was clear to him that many of his faculty colleagues would support any strategy that would help to save their jobs or those of their friends.

While Chris was not personally worried about being laid off, he did have two younger friends in the science department who might well be vulnerable. Each of these individuals had less seniority than he, and they would be the first to go if there were cuts in the science faculty. The district's contract with teachers made it clear that it was seniority in a tenure area that would determine who would be laid off first. He was also aware that throughout the building a number of the teachers with the least experience were among the most popular with the students. The last thing he wanted for himself was to be perceived by others as being uncaring about fellow teachers losing their jobs.

On the other hand, he did strongly believe that educational technology was an important teaching tool. At the same time he was not sure anything he might say at the meeting would change anyone's mind. Still, he felt compelled to begin to look for some evidence that technology does make a difference. One of the first articles he came across was from *Education World*, titled "Assistive Technology Helps All Kids Learn." Although the article was referring to the current use of technology for special education students, the author was arguing that "assistive and adaptive technology tools enable *all* students to become active participants in the general classroom environment." In supporting the argument, the following technology innovations were listed:

- Speech recognition ("voice recognition") systems allow students to control their computer by simply speaking.
- Personal reading machines scan a printed page and instantaneously read the page out loud.

- Talking calculators recite numbers, symbols, or functions as keys are pressed. They also can read back answers to completed problems.
- Video description: Just as captioning provides additional text for the hearing impaired, an additional narrative track describing on-screen action in videos enables blind and low-vision students to participate.

Along with these he found in the same article a list of "other long-standing and effective" technologies:

- Large print/screen modification hardware and software function like magnifying glasses, automatically moving over a page. That allows visually impaired students to more easily read textbooks, magazines, maps, charts, or fine print.
- Assistive listening devices transmit and amplify sounds to hearing impaired students. Students who experience difficulty processing auditory information might also benefit from using these devices.
- Captioning displays text transcription of auditory information on a screen (such as a television screen or LCD). Captioning allows hearing-impaired viewers to follow spoken dialogue or narration by reading text.[4]

This information might be helpful in allowing his fellow teachers to know some of the future technological possibilities for their classroom, but what he was really looking for was evidence that technology helped to increase the academic achievement of students. Although he found anecdotal accounts of districts that had invested heavily in computers and as a result claimed positive test results, he found no major studies of the scope of the Star Study to prove his argument. The more he read the clearer it became to him how difficult it might be to prove that computers or any other education technology really improved student learning.

One source said that the effort to prove the positive effects of technology would require researchers to carry out studies on a large scale. For example, it would be almost impossible to have a research project that had one group of students exposed to computers while another control group was not allowed to use them. It would be extremely difficult to find a school district that would allow such a study. He did find an author who asked her readers whether the effectiveness of technology should be measured solely by test scores or if schools should consider how exposure to technology prepared young people for future jobs.

If he could not match the class-size research and if his fellow teachers were willing to save jobs even if it meant sacrificing educational technology, Chris expected that he would be on the losing side of any argument that forced a choice between teachers and machines. It also occurred to him that even though the teachers union might urge a reduction in the technology budget, it was very possible that the administration and the board of education would not be sympathetic to such a recommendation. Daryl Franklin, the superintendent, had long been an advocate of educational technology, and the board of education included an engineer and an architect who might well support the technology budget. Still, the teachers union had always been an influential group within the district, and they might well seek additional public support for saving teachers' jobs. As far as the community was concerned, Chris was not sure how they would see the issue.

As he thought about the potential conflict, it occurred to him that there might well be other areas of the budget where cuts could be made. He had never looked carefully at his school district's budget, but perhaps now was a good time to consider all the possibilities. On his way home from school that night he stopped to pick up a copy of last year's school budget.

DISCUSSION QUESTIONS

1. Assuming that Chris attempts to defend the technology budget at the union meeting, what arguments should he use to try to offset the group's support for cutting the technology budget?
2. What do you feel should be the appropriate policy for the use of cell phones in school?
3. Are there other areas of a school budget that you might consider reducing before considering reductions in faculty or in technology?
4. If you were a member of the district's teachers union, what input might you offer at the meeting?

NOTES

1. Thomas, "Cell Phones—Time to Lift the Ban on Mobiles in the School Setting?" *Open Education,* www.openeducation.net/2009/02/08/cell-phone-time-to-lift-the-ban-on-mobiles-in-the-classroom (accessed February 13, 2009).

2. M. Richtel and B. Stone, "Technology," *New York Times*, February 15, 2009, www. nytimes.com/2009/02/26/technology/16phone.html (accessed February 19, 2009).

3. J. Johnson, D. Musial, G. Hall, D. Gollnick, and V. Dupuis. *Introduction to the Foundations of American Education*, thirteenth ed. (Boston: Allyn & Bacon, 2005), 146.

4. "Assistive Technology Helps All Kids Learn," *Education World*, August 9, 2005, www.education-world.com/a_tech/tech/tech220.shtml (accessed February 13, 2009).

ADDITIONAL RESOURCES

Briggs, L. "Using Classroom Clickers to Engage Every Student." *Campus Technology* (September 24, 2008). www.campustechnology.com/Articles/2008/09/Using-Classroom-Clickers-To-Engage-Every-Student.aspx.

Brown, M. D. "Handhelds in the Classroom." *Education World* (2001). www. education-world.com/a_tech/tech083.shtml.

Foltos, L. "Technology and Academic Achievement." *New Horizons for Learning* (2002). www.newhorizons.org/strategies/technology/foltos.htm.

What to Do about Facebook?

Online Communications Between Students and Teachers

Although Facebook, as well as the other popular social networks such as MySpace and Twitter, are relatively new, they have created some interesting issues. Facebook was launched in February 2004 by Mark Zuckerberg as a social network for Harvard students. By 2006 the program had grown to the point where Yahoo offered Zuckerberg $1 billion for the company.[1]

In January 2009, seventy million people were using the service. Although it began as a way for college students to communicate with their friends, it now includes users of all ages.[2] In just the last several years large numbers of high school students have joined the network. Membership for high school students is easier as most schools "generally do not issue email addresses, and so there is no requirement for an active .edu email account. Current high school members can invite others. Once you start college, you have the opportunity to change the account over to whatever school you attend."[3]

The Elmbrook School District in Wisconsin "has banned all chatter between Elmbrook staff and students on instant messaging or networking applications not sponsored by the district."[4] Other districts are considering similar measures, but most have yet to address the issue. In these schools it is often left up to the teacher's discretion as to what social networking interaction is appropriate between themselves and their students.

Andrew Meddler was twenty-two years old and a first-year high school social studies teacher. The first three months of his teaching career had gone quite smoothly. He was able to earn the respect of his students even though he had been quite strict in his classroom management methods. The fact that he was six foot three and weighed almost two hundred pounds certainly may have helped him to maintain order in his classroom. Although several of his students had sought to become closer to him socially, he had been able to establish an appropriate professional relationship with the members of his classes. This had been a challenge, as he was only four or five years older than some of his students. Still, Andrew had been able to communicate easily with his students about popular music and sports. On the whole, he was quite satisfied with his transition from college student to teacher.

Although he was no longer in college, he had clung to one habit from his days as a student. Almost every evening he took time to interact with a number of his college friends on Facebook. While he had accumulated a large network of friends, he was shocked one evening when he received a message from one of the students in his senior economics class.

The girl who sent the message, Caleigh Stevens, was a quiet member of the class. She seldom participated in discussions but always seemed attentive. He had thought of her as a slightly above average student. Her message on Facebook merely said that she was sorry, but she would not be in school the next day to take the test that was scheduled. Her two-sentence message referred to "family issues" as a reason for her absence. Without thinking much about it, Andrew quickly sent her a brief return message saying that she could take a make-up test the following Monday after school.

When Caleigh came to take the test, Andrew asked her if things were okay with her family. She merely stated, "Not really, but I did study for the test." It seemed obvious to Andrew that she did not want to discuss her family issue and he did not press her to talk about it. When she finished the test, they spoke briefly and she seemed to be a bit livelier. He felt that she was leaving his classroom in a better mood, and he did not think any more about Caleigh until he went to his computer that evening.

What he found was an extended message from her on Facebook. It began with a statement that she felt she owed him an explanation for having missed the class when the test was given. Caleigh then went on to explain that her parents had been quarreling often and that last week they had decided on a divorce. As an only child, she was extremely close to both of her parents, and the news that they were breaking up devastated her. This was despite the fact that her mother and father had assured her that they would still be as close as ever. This seemed impossible to her, especially since her father was taking a job in another state. They had also pointed out to her that she would soon be off to college and beginning a new life away from home. This had not made her feel any better, as she was already nervous about leaving home for college. Caleigh ended the message saying how alone and afraid she felt.

After reading the entire message twice, Andrew too was depressed by what his student was feeling. Having experienced a divorce in his own family while in high school, he could feel sincere empathy for what Caleigh was experiencing. In an effort to offer encouragement, he responded to her message by sharing his own family experience and how he had been able to remain close to both parents. He also mentioned that he had actually become closer to his father since the family had broken apart. He sent off the message without thinking whether or not it was wise for a teacher to share his personal life with a student. His goal had been to help encourage her through a difficult time. Beyond that, he had not thought about the implications of the correspondence he was now involved in.

The next evening the issue escalated as he received a third Facebook message from Caleigh, accompanied by a "friend request." This time it began with "Dear Andrew." The fact that she was calling him by his first name quickly raised a red flag in his mind as he read on. She began her message by thanking him for "sharing his personal story." The fact that he had experienced a situation similar to her own and had still prospered had been an encouragement to her. It was good to know that he had survived to become a "mature and caring teacher, and it helps me to believe that I too can overcome this life-shattering disappointment."

Caleigh went on to say that "having someone to talk to about my family has made it easier." She explained that she had no real close friends at school to talk with. It was the final paragraph that most disturbed Andrew. She had closed the note by writing the following:

I have not had any real boyfriends. Watching my parents' marriage fall apart has made me question having a lasting relationship of my own. How has your experience affected you? I don't know if you have a girlfriend. If you do, she is very lucky. On the other hand, if you don't. . . . Caleigh

Andrew wondered if what he had thought was simple encouragement had crossed the line into an ethically gray area. What if his principal, Mr. Sullivan, heard about the exchange on Facebook? He thought about a panel discussion of school administrators he had attended in college. One superintendent had reported that he had checked out teacher applicants on Facebook before he offered them a job. Andrew was not sure whether his current principal even knew what Facebook was, but he did know that other faculty members were active in using it. Beyond that, he was not sure if his school district had any policy regarding how teachers were to communicate with students. What he did know was that he had started something with Caleigh that he would have to deal with.

DISCUSSION QUESTIONS

1. Do you suppose that as a classroom teacher you will sometimes be party to the personal problems of your students? When this occurs, what is the appropriate role for a teacher?
2. Should school districts develop policies governing appropriate ways for teachers to communicate with students?
3. What should Andrew do about the correspondence that he has started with Caleigh?

NOTES

1. "Facebook," *Crunchbase*, June 25, 2008, www.crunchbase.com/company/facebook (accessed March 3, 2009).

2. "Traffic Analytics," *Crunchbase*, June 25, 2008, www.crunchbase.com/company/facebook (accessed March 3, 2009).

3. "85% of College Students Use Facebook," *Techcrunch*, www.techcrunch.com/2005/09/07/85-of-college-students-use-faceboook.html (accessed March 3, 2009).

4. L. Barack, "WI Schools Ban Facebook, IM Fraternizing Between Staff, Students," *School Library Journal*, February 23, 2009, www.schoollibraryjournal.com/index.asp?layout=talkbackcommentsfull.html (accessed February 25, 2009).

ADDITIONAL RESOURCES

Carter, H., T. Foulger, and A. Ewbank. "Have You Googled Your Teacher Lately? Teachers' Use of Social Networking Sites." *Phi Delta Kappan* 89, no. 9 (May 1,

WHAT TO DO ABOUT FACEBOOK?

2008): 681–85. (ERIC Document Reproduction Service No. EJ794356.) Retrieved April 15, 2009, from ERIC database.

MacFarlane, M. "Misbehavior in Cyberspace." *School Administrator* 64, no. 9 (October 1, 2007): 4–8. (ERIC Document Reproduction Service No. EJ777118.) Retrieved April 15, 2009, from ERIC database.

Simon, M. "Online Student-Teacher Friendships Can Be Tricky." *CNN.org* (August 13, 2008). www.cnn.com/2008/TECH/08/12/studentsteachers.online/index.html.

I Should Have Had a Rubric

Assigning Grades in Performance-Based Music Classes

Assigning grades to students in classes such as instrumental music and physical education can be challenging. To a lesser degree, the same is true in some art classes. A teacher must weigh factors such as effort, skill, and improvement or growth. Should a talented musician or artist receive high grades based on their natural ability or should other factors be considered in assessing such students? Because grades in these classes almost always affect a student's grade point average, teachers must devise defendable plans for assigning grades. Failure to do so can lead to charges of favoritism or a lack of professionalism.

Greg Cho vaguely remembered hearing about using rubrics to assign grades in his education classes in college. He now had to admit to himself that these classes were not a high priority during his collegiate career. As a jazz saxophonist, his primary interest had been in classes dealing with music theory and arrangement along with playing in the jazz and wind ensembles. Whenever possible, he had also spent many evenings playing professionally in a number of locations. He looked back fondly at performing with a jazz quartet in a number of bars and coffeehouses.

Despite his lack of real interest in his education classes, Greg was truly enjoying his first teaching position. He considered himself extremely fortunate to be selected as the senior high band director in the Seneca Valley School District. Most of his fellow instrumental music education graduates had been hired for teaching positions at the elementary or middle school level. For him, the job at Seneca Valley was perfect in that he enjoyed the older students and was able to teach them some rather advanced music, including several of the arrangements that he had written in college.

His first semester as a teacher had flown by and, in his mind, it had gone very well. Most of the students were a pleasure to work with, and they seemed to enjoy his teaching methods. The fact that he was only a few years older than many of his students seemed to help him to communicate easily with them. On the other hand, there was no question that conducting a band of eighty senior high students presented a challenge. Greg found that keeping his percussion section from disturbing rehearsals was difficult. Too often, when they had rests written in their music, the percussionists would carry on a conversation or fuss with their equipment. There were also several woodwind players who tended to play out of tune. This was especially true of his two oboe players, who seldom sounded very good when playing together. The trombone section sometimes got carried away, and they could almost drown out the entire band. Still, for the most part, he was pleased with the musical progress the group was making.

One of his problem students was Schuyler Fairchild, a senior who sat in the second chair in the trumpet section. Schuyler was a young man who seemed to do well in every area of school life. He was an honor student and the captain of the basketball team. However, Greg found him to be less than friendly and suspected that he really wanted to be in the first chair of his section. Unfortunately, even though he was a senior, in terms of ability and dedication he could not match Tai Kato. Tai, as a sophomore, was perhaps the most talented and hardworking musician in the band. Whenever there was a trumpet solo, he learned it quickly and always played it perfectly.

Perhaps as a result of not being the top player in his section, Schuyler seemed to lack any sense of commitment to music. At one of his sectional lessons, he had admitted that he did not have time to practice. During rehearsals he was not always attentive, and it had been necessary on several occasions to ask him to stop talking with Erin Mosckivich, who sat on his left in the trumpet section. On two separate occasions he had missed band rehearsal and when asked about his absence, he had merely told Greg that he had been talking with the basketball coach. Despite several efforts to become friendly with the boy, his teacher had found him somewhat distant.

On his report card for the first quarter Schuyler had received a B+, which he told Greg was the lowest grade he had received that quarter. The B+ grade had brought about no change in his effort and attitude during the second quarter. If anything, it seemed to Greg that his student was less interested, and his less-than-positive attitude was beginning to become evident to other members of the band. When compared to his other students, Greg found his trumpet player to be almost arrogant, and at times even somewhat disrespect- ful. As the second quarter ended, it seemed to him that another B+ on the report card would be an undeserved gift. As a result Greg decided to make a point, and he gave Schuyler a C for his band grade.

It was this C grade that had created his dilemma. Greg had received an e- mail from his principal, Amanda Lewis, who informed him that he was to join her at 3:30 on Friday for a meeting with Schuyler's parents to discuss the grade that he had received in band. Mrs. Lewis asked Greg to come to her office at 3:00 to talk about the grade. The problem had become significant when the guidance department had announced the top ten students in the senior class. These students would be honored at graduation, and their names and pictures would be published in the local newspaper. Although Schuyler had been num- ber ten in the class at the beginning of the second quarter, because of two of his grades he had dropped to number eleven. The parents were meeting with the two teachers who had given their son lower grades on the second quarter report card. The e-mail from his principal said that Greg should be prepared to defend the grade, because it was clear that the Fairchild family was upset.

For Greg, the problem was that he was not sure how to best defend the grade in question. In his class book he had kept attendance and did have Schuyler down for two unexcused absences. Other than that, he had no paper record to rely on. At the first band rehearsal, he had told his students that they would be graded on participation, effort, and attendance, but he had not defined the terms or assigned a percentage value to any of them. With the exception of two unexcused absences, all he had was his subjective judgment that Schuyler had not practiced his trumpet or given his best effort, and that at times he had been somewhat disruptive.

On hearing about his meeting with the Fairchilds, Greg asked his friend Joy Schillanger, who was an art teacher, for her thoughts on how to defend the grade. Joy talked about the rubric that she used for art projects and how she assigned a percentage of the grade for specific categories. For each project, she would give the students clear instructions, and they would be graded on how well they met the requirements of the project. Although Joy shared with him a sample art project rubric, it was not especially helpful to Greg. He also talked with another friend in the physical education department and found that even in physical education there were preordained factors that were used as the basis for a grade. This was occurring even though the physical education teacher was working with more than the eighty students Greg had in his band.

While he had not developed a specific grading system, it occurred to Greg that maybe it was not too late to create such a system. Thinking about this alternative, it seemed to him that to create a system after he had marked the report cards would be unethical. In addition, he would have to rig any rubric to make certain that all of his students received the grade he had put on their cards. He would have to think long and hard about what he was going to say to Mrs. Lewis and to Mr. and Mrs. Fairchild. He could not help but think that he should have had a rubric.

DISCUSSION QUESTIONS

1. What are the factors that might be considered in developing a grade for students in a band, orchestra, or chorus? List the factors that might be used by an art teacher in grading an assignment. Finally, what should physical education instructors consider in assigning grades in their program?
2. Using a percentage system, design a grading rubric for one of the three classes mentioned in question one.
3. How should Greg deal with his current grading dilemma?

ADDITIONAL RESOURCES

Brown, L. C. *Checking Progress with Checklists*. MENC: The National Association for Music Education (January 22, 2009). www.menc.org/v/general_music /checking-progress-with-checklists.

Chiodo, P. "Assessing a Cast of Thousands." *Music Educators Journal* 87, no. 6 (May 2001): 17. Retrieved April 15, 2009, from Academic Search Premier database.

"Resources for Assessing Music Students." *Teaching Music* (December 2004). Retrieved April 15, 2009, from Professional Development Collection database.

The Unruly Class

What to Do When Your Classroom Management Plan Isn't Working

Even experienced teachers sometimes have classes that provide special challenges. Often it is the unique makeup of the group that makes certain classes difficult to manage. This is especially true when there are conflicts between students within the classroom. If the group contains cliques of students, the problem can be even worse. A situation such as this can be further aggravated if the students have divided themselves by race or by gang membership. In such situations the traditional behavior management techniques may not prove to be effective.

Chrissy Kaleta was in the final year of her probationary period as an English teacher in Eastwood Middle School. Her first two years in the school had been without incident, and she felt that she was well on her way to earning tenure. This was her second teaching position, as she had spent four years in a district in a neighboring state. There she had earned tenure and had only changed schools when her husband had taken a new job.

Classroom management had never been a serious problem for Chrissy in either of her schools. The fact that she had an outgoing personality along with the capacity to plan engaging lessons had helped her to become a well-liked and respected member of the faculty in both of her schools. Unfortunately, this year her seventh-period English class had been causing her sleepless nights.

To analyze the reasons that this group failed to respond to her usual methods of classroom management, she had attempted to analyze the students in the class. It occurred to her that one of the major problems seemed to center on two cliques of girls who were unable to get along. The problem was made more difficult because one of the groups was made up of African American students, and the other clique was all Hispanic. On numerous occasions there were times when the two groups engaged in name calling and threats. The language the students used during these verbal exchanges included such words as "retard," "pervert," and even "whore." On two occasions fights had broken out between the two rival groups. Chrissy had been able to stop them before anyone was hurt and had decided not to send the students to the office.

Her decision to avoid using the administration to solve her discipline problems was based on the fact that she had always handled classroom disturbances by herself. In addition, she was worried that relying on the assistant principal to keep order in her class might cause the students to lose any respect they might have for her. On the other hand, Chrissy was not sure she had been successful in earning the respect of many of the students.

There were several other girls who were not a part of these two groups. One of them was extremely quiet and kept to herself. Another was sometimes a victim of bullying by other members of the class. Chrissy had heard her called a "nerd," and on one occasion the girl had hinted that she might be the victim of cyberbullying. When questioned about this, however, the student had chosen not to confide in her.

While the girls were difficult, the boys in the class presented a different type of challenge. Jeremy Decluxe was a foot taller and weighed twenty-five pounds more than anyone else in the seventh-grade class. The boy was even taller than his teacher. Because he was repeating seventh grade, Jeremy was also a year older than most of the other students. None of the other boys dared challenge his physical domination in the classroom. Several times he had quickly subdued any boy who dared to question him. Most often he was quiet in class, but he did not hesitate to tell other students to "shut their mouths." There was little question in Chrissy's mind that the other students were more afraid of Jeremy than they were of her.

With a couple of exceptions, the young men in the class were overly talkative and too often could be heard using inappropriate language in their conversations with each other. Hardly a class went by when Chrissy was not forced to stop instruction to deal with unruly students. The improper language even crept into informal class discussions. If there was a difference of opinion between students during a class, some of the students quickly resorted to name calling.

Almost daily it took several minutes for Chrissy to get the group to settle down. Near the end of the period, which was also the end of the school day, most of the students would shut down five minutes before the final bell. On several occasions when she was truly able to engage them in the lesson, she was able to keep their attention for the entire period, but this was infrequent. The most disturbing part about the class was that a half-dozen of the students really wanted to learn, and in Chrissy's mind these children were being cheated because so much class time was being spent on management issues.

Although Chrissy was not a teacher who was comfortable yelling, she found herself doing so as it was often difficult to be heard over the voices of the students. She was not a person who became angry often, but increasingly she was finding herself upset during the class and she had even resorted to making cynical comments to her students. It had reached the point where she was dreading her seventh-period class. They seemed so involved in their own worlds that English class was not something most of them seemed to care about.

When Chrissy was honest with herself, she knew that she could use help managing the group. As a proud teacher, she had avoided admitting to her colleagues that she was having trouble. Because it was the final year of her probation, she was also seeking to deal with her problems by herself. Her concern was that she did not want the administration to know she was having disciplinary problems. A number of times, she had almost referred a student to the office, but had always held back rather than making an issue out of a student's behavior. At the same time, she was beginning to doubt that she could make it through the year with this group.

One idea Chrissy had considered was that she should introduce some sort of positive incentive system to reward good behavior. She had resisted trying this because it seemed to her that it was merely bribing her students to be good. While she had listed her behavior expectations for the students during the first week of classes, it appeared that currently the students were paying less and less attention to the rules she had announced. Too often they seemed much more involved with their personal issues and their conflicts with each other than with her lessons.

This had been especially true yesterday, when she had been forced to interrupt the lesson numerous times in order to quiet the group. Talking out of turn was a constant problem, but even worse was the way the students treated each other. Chrissy could not help but think that the class included an inordinate number of unhappy and angry kids who did not like each other. She also had to admit that many of them were not intimidated by their teacher. For Chrissy, it had seemed last night that she had reached the point where she needed to do something about her seventh-period class.

DISCUSSION QUESTIONS

1. Have you ever been in a class where student behavior made it difficult for the instructor to teach? Was the teacher ever able to improve the situation? If so, how?
2. What are the behaviors that should cause a teacher to send a student to the office for additional discipline?
3. What do you think Chrissy should do about her difficult class?

ADDITIONAL RESOURCES

Kafka, J. "Sitting on a Tinderbox: Racial Conflict, Teacher Discretion, and the Centralization of Disciplinary Authority." *American Journal of Education* 144, no 3 (May 1, 2008): 247–70. (ERIC Document Reproduction Service No. EJ790973.) Retrieved April 16, 2009, from ERIC database.

Muscott, H., E. Mann, and M. LeBrun. "Positive Behavioral Interventions and Supports in New Hampshire: Effects of Large-Scale Implementation of Schoolwide Positive Behavior Support on Student Discipline and Academic Achievement." *Journal of Positive Behavior Interventions* 10, no. 3 (January 1, 2008): 190–205. (ERIC Document Reproduction Service No. EJ798463.) Retrieved April 16, 2009, from ERIC database.

Sadler, C., and G. Sugai. "Effective Behavior and Instructional Support: A District Model for Early Identification and Prevention of Reading and Behavior Problems." *Journal of Positive Behavior Interventions* 11, no. 1 (January 1, 2009): 35–46. (ERIC Document Reproduction Service No. EJ821403.) Retrieved April 16, 2009, from ERIC database.

About the Author

Bill Hayes has been a high school social studies teacher, department chair, assistant principal, and high school principal. From 1973 to 1994, he served as superintendent of schools for the Byron-Bergen Central School District, which is located eighteen miles west of Rochester, New York. During his career, he was an active member of the New York State Council of Superintendents and is the author of a council publication titled *The Superintendency: Thoughts for New Superintendents,* which is used to prepare new superintendents in New York state.

Mr. Hayes has also written a number of articles for various educational journals. After retiring from the superintendency he served as chair of the Teacher Education Division at Roberts Wesleyan College in Rochester, New York, until 2003. He currently remains a full-time teacher at Roberts Wesleyan. During the past ten years he has written twelve books, which have all been published by Scarecrow Education Press and R&L Education. They include *Real-Life Case Studies for School Administrators, Real-Life Case Studies for Teachers, So You Want to Be a Superintendent?, So You Want to Be a School Board Member?, Real-Life Case Studies for School Board Members, So You Want to Become a College Professor?, So You Want to Become a Principal?, Are We Still a Nation at Risk Two Decades Later?, Horace Mann's Vision of the Public Schools: Is It Still Relevant?, The Progressive Education Movement: Is It Still a Factor in Today's Schools?, All New Real-Life Case Studies for Administrators,* and *No Child Left Behind: Past, Present, and Future.*

Made in the USA
Monee, IL
16 January 2021